AN ENGLISHWOMAN'S GARDEN

Mrs. LOUDON'S

GARDENING

FOR

LADIES.

H. CORBOULD

AN ENGLISHWOMAN'S GARDEN

HELEN PENN

BBC BOOKS

ACKNOWLEDGEMENTS

I am indebted to P.M. Pictures Ltd for suggesting that I write this book and for making their transcripts available.

Like all writers about gardening I must also acknowledge my debt to the Royal Horticultural Society's Lindley Library. The staff could not be more helpful and the library itself is a pleasure to work in.

My editors at the BBC have been considerate and practical and all an author could wish for and I am grateful for their support.

I would like to thank Chrissie Tuta, my friend and gardening companion of many years. We have visited hundreds of gardens and nurseries, gone on courses together and shared gardening books. Many of the ideas in this book arose from our discussions. Without this stimulus, the book would never have been written, and my gardening would have been a much duller affair.

In a book like this, largely based on interviews, errors are inevitable, although we have tried very hard to avoid them. I hope that they are not serious, and that where they occur, they can be overlooked.

This book is published to accompany the television series entitled *An Englishwoman's Garden* which was produced by P.M. Pictures Ltd for the BBC. The series was produced and directed by Ann Lalić and the Series Producer was Penny Forster. It was first broadcast in Autumn 1993.

Published by BBC Books,
a division of BBC Enterprises Limited,
Woodlands, 80 Wood Lane,
London W12 0TT

First published 1993
Text copyright © P.M. Pictures Ltd and Helen Penn 1993
The moral rights of the author have been asserted
All rights reserved
ISBN 0 563 36430 0

Set in 12/16 pt Baskerville by Ace Filmsetting Ltd, Frome, Somerset
Printed and bound in Great Britain by BPCC Paulton Books Ltd, Paulton
Colour separation by Technik Ltd, Berkhamsted
Jacket printed by Belmont Press Ltd, Northampton

FRONTISPIECE
The title page for the Victorian best-seller
Mrs Louden's Gardening for Ladies.

CONTENTS

FOREWORD

by PENELOPE HOBHOUSE

An Englishwoman's Garden touches on the gardening lives of women from all walks of life, stressing how, often unsung and unrecorded, they indulged their passion for plants and flowers. Helen Penn reveals how much the history of English gardening has depended on women. In the Middle Ages English queens extended gardening practice: Queen Eleanor of Castile introduced gardeners and the hollyhock from thirteenth-century Spain; Queen Philippa of Hainault introduced rosemary in 1338 and commissioned a treatise on its properties. By the early seventeenth century housewives had become the audience for practical manuals by writers such as Thomas Hill, Thomas Tusser and William Lawson. It was the woman's job to sort seeds, preserve fruit and collect and distil herbs – demanding and skilful tasks on which a family's comfort depended. Meanwhile, the humblest women were being employed as weeders to work in the gardens of the wealthy for a few pence an hour.

Through succeeding centuries Helen Penn traces women as great garden patrons, archivists, botanical illustrators, owners of nurseries and amateur gardeners. Victorian ladies excelled in gardening but, fashions change and it was Edwardians such as Gertrude Jekyll who put flower gardening on to an artistic level with painting, establishing a new English gardening style. The eminently quotable Miss Jekyll, trained as a painter, recommended using plants 'that they shall form beautiful pictures' and encouraged application 'in which it becomes a point of honour to be always striving for the best'. She gave women gardeners a boost into the twentieth century, during which they have excelled in all fields of creative and ecological gardening.

As practical gardening becomes more technical and in some ways more male-orientated (how many women are interested in the latest machinery or in the legal mysteries of chemical warfare on disease and pests?) Helen Penn, without showing more than a degree of feminine chauvinism, demonstrates how women influence the aesthetics of the profession. Serious, intuitive, thorough, attentive to detail and above all plantlovers, women remain deeply involved in lifting gardening from the commonplace 'to rank as a fine art'.

Penelope Hobhouse
Tintinhull
March 1993

INTRODUCTION

T his book is not about what to do in the garden. It does not contain any gardening tips except, perhaps, indirectly. Readers concerned with the tribulations of gardening – slugs, smelly compost, builders' rubble, dandelions and clover in the lawn, black spot on the roses, worms in the carrots, dry summers and wet winters, and all the other pitfalls – will not find solutions here. Nor is the book about plants, although it easily could have been. The story of gardening in Britain is in large measure about the acquisition and distribution of plants. People have gone to extraordinary lengths to obtain plants from abroad, to propagate, grow and display them and, for that matter, to write about and draw them. Most of the plants grown in Britain originate from somewhere else in the world.

The book *is* about people who make gardens – in particular about women who make gardens. Gardening is an extraordinarily popular hobby in Britain, and its devotees are men and women from all classes and all walks of life. The reasons why it is so popular are complex, and vary from the psychological and the sociological to the purely horticultural. However, it is not fanciful to claim that although men have made more of a career of it, gardening is above all a woman's passion. Women have excelled as gardeners, although they have not always been given the credit they deserve for doing so, and they have often been discouraged – as in many other fields – from exercising their talents. Whatever the history books conventionally tell us, the evidence of women's interest, faint as it sometimes appears, can be traced a long way back.

The American poet and novelist Alice Walker suggests in her book of essays *In Search of Our Mothers' Gardens* that her mother, who lived in dire poverty for

A Lutyens–Jekyll garden at Upton Grey in Hampshire, showing *Clematis montana* arching behind a stone wall, framing stachys and a stone seat.

most of her life, gardened because it was the only way she had left open to her to be creative, to express herself as an artist. Her life as a cotton picker and as mother and provider for eight children left her little time or energy, but gardening was as necessary to her as breathing. She got up very early to draw water from the well to tend the flowers; she worked at back-breaking tasks in the fields, came home and cooked and cleaned, and at the tail end of the evening, until it was too dark to see, she worked again in the garden, digging, replanting, pruning, doing whatever jobs were needed.

> . . . when my mother is working in her flowers . . . she is radiant, almost to the point of being invisible − except as Creator; hand and eye. She is involved in the work her soul must have. Ordering the universe in the image of her personal conception of beauty.

This is the evidence that is usually missing; the lives of women, except those of the richest and most powerful, were unremittingly hard and largely unrecorded until recent times. Because there are so few records, it is easy to suppose that this energy and passion, this reverence for the beauty of flowers and the growth of plants, and concern for their arrangement, is a new phenomenon. The history of gardening is often presented as if it is the story of rich landowners employing the leading designers of their day to landscape large tracts of earth according to the latest artistic fashion; mounds, parterres, mazes, topiary, lakes, and allées with classical statues coyly sited at the far end.

Gardening is much more prosaic and personal than this kind of top-down history implies. This book outlines some of the processes of gardening, and how they have influenced women; or, in the last century and a half, how influential women have been in their impact upon gardening life. Gardening is a domestic activity often slotted in with other household tasks. It is also one of the few spheres where amateurs and professionals mix freely, and where the transition from one to the other is accomplished with relative ease. This is another reason why women have become so prominent as gardeners − they have not been inhibited by professional barriers and can slip into expertise without having had to make their way up a career ladder.

Gardening is eclectic; it is open to everyone who has a backyard or a balcony with pots or even an allotment; it is not limited to those with know-how or space or money or reputation. Anyone can try it. Gardening is also cumulative: it takes a long time to build up the practical knowledge of how different plants grow in different sites, and how to display them to best advantage to create a work of living art. As Gertrude Jekyll once remarked,

> Those who do not know are apt to think that hardy flower gardening of the best kind is easy. It is not easy at all. It has taken me half a life-time merely to find out what is best worth doing, and a good slice of the other half to puzzle out ways of doing it.

Enthusiasm, endeavour and persistence, as well as talent, are the chief characteristics of the women who appear in this book. Many of these women are in their seventies and eighties, having discovered gardening as they got older. Gardening is often an adventure of middle and old age, a means of expanding one's horizons at a time when other options begin to shrink.

There are all kinds of well-springs for garden making. The book considers some of them: the story of the gardening schools and how women benefited from them; the influence of family example and tradition; the urge to conserve flowers and habitats which are fast being eroded; the nurseries; the garden societies and clubs; the botanical artists and the garden journalists who record and inspire. This may sound like a hotchpotch, and perhaps it is a little, but no more so than the real world in which all these activities go on. The boundaries of gardening are fluid, and the book reflects some of this diversity.

An Englishwoman's Garden explores why women garden and what motivates them. It looks at the fruits of their labour, at some of the magnificent gardens they have made, and at their broader contribution to the gardening scene. It takes a historical as well as a contemporary perspective, and it draws upon a variety of material, including books and magazines, letters and diaries, engravings, photographs and other records from the past; and upon the memories and opinions of those living and gardening now.

In one sense the book is unjust. The selection of the women who appear in it is arbitrary. Those portrayed do not necessarily represent the best, although some are justifiably famous. There have been many who have been left out. To be fair, this book should have been a small encyclopaedia. Instead it offers a taste of the art; a glimpse of what gardening can give.

11

CHAPTER ONE

WOMEN WEEDERS, VICTORIAN STRAITJACKETS

Lady Alicia Amherst, self-effacing, hard-working and very thorough, described herself as 'a citizen and gardener of London'. Her book, *A History of Gardening in England*, first published nearly 100 years ago, is a classic. She was exceptionally well informed – she hunted out dusty Elizabethan and Jacobean manuscripts and household accounts to glean extra information about how plants were ordered and gardeners were paid. She had some interesting insights about gardening history. She wrote so well that her book has hardly dated. She dedicated the book to her mother.

I should like to record that I learnt all my practical knowledge of gardening as a child from my mother, who had always been devoted to gardening long years before it was considered a fashionable past-time for ladies.

How to be decorous whilst watering and deadheading.
An illustration from *Mrs Mackarness' Young Lady's Book*, 1876.

An early photograph of Lady Alicia Amherst, scholarly historian, traveller, botanist, philanthropist, and 'citizen and gardener of London'.

Lady Alicia had several other advantages besides learning to use a trowel at her mother's knee. Her father had a priceless collection of early gardening books in his library, and she browsed as a child through Thomas Tusser's *A hundreth good pointes of husbandrie* (1557); John Gerard's *The Herball* (1597); William Lawson's *Countrie Houswifes Garden* (1617); Thomas Hyll's *The Gardeners-Labyrinth* (1577); and, most famous of all, John Parkinson's seventeenth-century state of the art book on gardening, *Paradisi in Sole Paradisus Terrestris* (1629). These books are all now reprinted in modern editions but when Lady Alicia read them they were collector's pieces.

As well as coming from a gardening family, Lady Alicia was an active plant collector in her own right. She accompanied her husband on trips to Mozambique, Rhodesia, Ceylon, Australia, New Zealand and Canada, and botanized in each of them. She had philanthropic leanings, and her last book was a meticulously detailed review of London parks and open spaces, and a discussion of how they might be made more accessible to children.

Lady Alicia is one of many women who have had an impact on gardening.

The view she put forward in her book was that gardening history mirrored the times; 'The history of the Gardens of England follows step by step the history of the people.' She showed how the wider world affected the status and styles of gardening; colonial expansion, industrial change, war and peace, taxes and transport, all shaped how we have made gardens, raised, displayed and used plants. Women have always been gardeners, but the nature and visibility of their contribution have varied. In this century, more than in any other, women have influenced gardening styles, but the records of their involvement go back a long way.

Women gardeners have frequently been under-rated, but not everyone feels quite so strongly about it as Eleanor Perényi, an American gardening writer. In an article called 'A Woman's Place' (1981) she writes of 'flower-filled ghettos' and argues that the contribution of women has been falsely portrayed in gardening literature, as in other spheres, and women have been made to appear simperingly sweet and rather dopey. She makes a convincing case by quoting the gratuitous advice given to women gardeners over the centuries. For instance, John Lawrence, writing in 1726, pompously pronounced:

> I flatter myself the ladies would soon think their vacant Hours in the Culture of the *Flower Garden* would be more innocently spent and with greater Satisfaction than the common Talk over a Tea Table where Envy and Detraction so commonly preside.

In medieval and early Tudor times gardens were productive rather than recreational, and most skilled gardeners came from religious orders. The monasteries and convents cultivated fruit and vegetables, and grew herbs for the infirmary.

A few early stories about women gardeners have filtered down. The Abbess Christina at Romsey, Hampshire, in 1092 grew roses and flowering herbs which William Rufus pretended he wanted to see in order to gain access to the nunnery (to abduct an heiress). Eleanor of Castile (the Queen of Edward I) brought a team of the best gardeners in the world from Moorish Spain to her garden in Hertfordshire in 1289. Queen Philippa of Hainault's mother commissioned a treatise on growing rosemary as a present for her daughter on the birth of her grandson, Lionel, in 1338. Otherwise, most of the other

Women weeders working alongside men in this scene from rural life by the sixteenth-century artist Jacob Grimmer.

records of women gardeners are of 'women weeders'. Some of the household accounts listed by Alicia Amherst show that working women were employed as casual labour to weed and do other light tasks in the garden, and were paid only a half or a third of men's rates.

When England became more prosperous and stable on the accession of the Tudors, it was possible to settle down to gardening more seriously. Two classic books, by Thomas Tusser and William Lawson, gave advice on the role of country housewives – for those who could read. In Tusser's book *A hundreth good pointes of husbandrie* the housewife's job was to feed the household; oversee the dairy; card and spin flax and hemp; look after the saffron crop; collect, clean, and save seeds; and above all to gather and distil herbs and fruit. The whole book is written in verse, and this frequently quoted extract gives a flavour of his writing:

> Wife into thy garden, and set me a plot
> With strawberry roots of the best to be got:
> Such growing abroad, among thorns in the wood,
> Well chosen and picked prove excellent good.

Tusser elaborates upon his advice in another book, *The pointes of Huswiferie united to the comfort of husband*. Households had to be self-sufficient in every respect, and women worked long and hard. Work began at four in summer and five in winter and involved a lot of feeding, cleaning and clearing up. At dusk she had to make sure nothing was left outside:

> No clothes in the garden, no trinkets without,
> No doore leeve unbolted for feare of a doubt.

In carrying out these tasks a housewife had to show 'unfailing cheerfulness' towards her husband; tiredness or childbearing was no excuse for slackness or impertinence. (Tusser's own wife appeared to be constantly ill, and lacked the energy to follow his routine.)

Sixty years later, in 1617, Lawson is more moderate in his instructions, and assumes more autonomy for the housewife and rather more help from the servants. In *Countrie Housewifes Garden* he gives practical advice on soil, siting of gardens, fencing, designs for herb and flower beds, and bee-keeping.

Twelve years after Lawson, John Parkinson published his *Paradisi in Sole Paradisus Terrestris*. This is one of the most beautiful, comprehensive and authoritative gardening books ever written. Parkinson was an apothecary, with widespread gardening connections. He was sent plants to try out from all over the world. His book acknowledges the supremacy of women in the flower garden; flowers for their own beautiful sake had by then become an established feature of the garden.

> And because there bee many Gentlewomen and others that would gladly have some fine flowers to furnish their Gardens, but know not what the

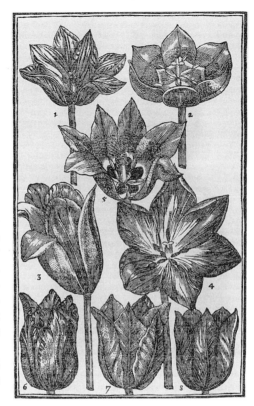

John Parkinson, the famous seventeenth-century gardener, described tulips as 'stately and delightful' and thought that every gentlewoman should grow them. This woodcut is taken from his book *Paradisi in Sole Paradisus Terrestris*, where he recorded more than 40 kinds of tulip.

names of those things are that they desire, nor what are the times of their flowring, nor the skill and knowledge of their right ordering, planting, displanting, transplanting and replanting; I have here for their sakes set downe the nature, times, and manner of ordering in a briefe manner.

He recommended daffodils, lilies 'especially crown imperials and martagons', hyacinths, crocus, anemones, flowerdeleuce (iris), gillyflowers (carnations, pinks and wallflowers) and, above all, tulips.

. . . besides this glory of variety in colors that these flowers have, they carry so stately and delightfull a forme and do abide so long in their bravery (enduring above three whole months from the first unto the last) that there is no Lady or Gentlewoman of any worth that is not caught with this delight, or not delighted with these flowers.

This echoes Dutch 'tulipomania' when tulip bulbs exchanged hands for hundreds of pounds each. Parkinson lists more than forty kinds of tulip, and even comments that the bulbs are nourishing and can be eaten, although the price makes it unwise to do so!

He comments on the origin of the plants he lists, and where they were collected if they were new introductions. Plants had begun to arrive from America and the Caribbean, and also from Eastern Europe. He lists one woman amongst his gardening correspondents. She sent him a lady's slipper orchid (which he groups with hellebores) and a double cardamine, which she had collected in the wild.

> I am enformed by a courteous Gentlewoman, a great lover of these delights, called Mistris Thomasin Tunstall, who dwelleth . . . neare Hornby Castle . . . and who hath often sent mee up the rootes to London which have borne faire flowers in my Garden.

He considers Mistress Tunstall sets a good example:

> . . . no doubt many things doe lye hid, and not observed which in time may bee discovered if our Country Gentlemen and Women and others in their severall places where they dwell, would bee more carefull and diligent.

A contemporary description exists of the garden of 'Goodwife Cantrey' in Northamptonshire – although it is unlikely that she read Parkinson. She grew double and single larkspurs, double and single sweet williams, three kinds of spiderwort, lupins in four colours, purple and white scabious, marigolds, life-everlasting, London pride, hollyhocks, and many other flowers. Her medicinal and herbal collection included fennel (for weak eyes), camomile (for head-aches), white lilies (to break bile), goat's rue (for plague) and double feverfew (against shaking fever).

Gardening books like that of Parkinson offered useful advice to the new middle classes who were educated enough to take advantage of them. But amongst the aristocracy there were some garden owners whose plans were on a very grand scale indeed. The ideas of renaissance Italy were being filtered through France and Flanders, and the leading exponent in Britain was a man called De Caus. He worked for Queen Anne of Denmark, the wife of James I, and in 1609 designed a huge geometric garden; and for Ann Clifford and her husband the Duke of Pembroke, he made a highly ornate garden on

An extravagantly formal and symmetrical Jacobean garden designed by De Caus showing parterres, tree-lined walks, statuary and a fountain.

the theme of 'love and homage to the Countess'. This garden had parterres with fountains and statuary; a wilderness presided over by Flora and Bacchus; and formal walks lined with cherry trees. Henrietta Maria, the Queen of Charles I, had her gardens at St James' Palace and at Wimbledon designed by a Frenchman, André Mollet, in a vast symmetrical design of parterres, a labyrinth and a wilderness.

Cromwell's puritanism was a revolt against aristocratic excesses, and the gardens of leading aristocrats could certainly be said to be excessive. The mid-seventeenth-century puritan emphasis was on husbandry, on honest toil, on the production of fruit and vegetables. After the Restoration, however, gardening became a respectable art again. John Evelyn, the late-seventeenth-century diarist, was a shrewd commentator of the time and a noted garden expert. He liked evergreen hedges, and had a huge holly hedge in his garden in Deptford. In his letters he writes about several well-known lady gardeners, Lady Brook in Hackney in 1654; Lady Clarendon in Swallowfield, Berkshire in 1685, who was 'extraordinarily skilled in the flowery part'; and Lady Fox, of whom he was rather critical.

> I went with my Lady Fox to survey her buildings and give some directions for the garden at Chiswick; . . . the garden much too narrow, the place without water, neere an highway . . . little land about it, so I wonder at the expense; but women will have their will.

John Evelyn's liking for evergreens caught on. A Chelsea firm, London and Wise, became the leading suppliers and sold topiary to everyone who wanted to be in fashion. No shape was too elaborate and every fashionable garden had at least a topiary peacock. This craze for topiary was soon parodied, by the poet Pope, who wrote a famous satirical verse on Adam and Eve clipped out of Irish yew. (Pope may have parodied the gardening fashion, but judging by engravings, his own garden was full of grotesque objects.)

In 1732 Philip Miller, the Curator of the newly established Chelsea Physic Garden, published his *Gardener's Dictionary*. He was at the centre of an influential group of gardeners and nurserymen who in 1730 formed the 'Society of Gardeners'. They met monthly at a coffee house to discuss the nomenclature and propagation of plants, 'Nature being various and intricate, and not to be discovered without diligent enquiry . . .'. Many new plants had been introduced since Parkinson's time and they wanted a record of them and where they could be obtained. In their manifesto they give credit to a number of contemporary gardeners, amongst whom was one woman,

> Her Grace the Dutchess of Beaufort did also collect a numerous Quantity of rare Plants into those famous Gardens of Badmington, where she preserved and maintained them with great Care in wonderful Beauty for many Years.

The first gardening book by a woman was prompted by this circle of gardeners. Elizabeth Blackwell was a gifted artist whose husband was in a debtors' prison. Hearing that the society was interested in an illustrated edition of plants, she moved to Chelsea, and produced in 1737 *A Curious Herbal*, '500 cuts of the most useful plants which are used in the Practice of Physik'. She not only drew the flowers but also engraved them on copper and coloured them herself. Her husband annotated the drawings from prison, and gave a description and a list of medicinal uses for each plant. The book sold and his debts were paid. A warm commendation from some of the Society's members appears in the frontispiece of the book:

> We whose names are underwritten, having seen a considerable number of the drawings from which the plates are to be engraved and likewise some of those coloured plates think it a justice done to the publik to declare our satisfaction with them, and our good opinion of the capacity of the Undertaker.

Despite this civilized accolade, Elizabeth Blackwell's book was the last of a genre. Herbals and gardening books were in decline. The reason for this was the 'landscape movement' or what is still called abroad '*le jardin anglais*'. Partly in reaction to the grotesque topiary of London and Wise, a new style of gardening had caught on. This involved grand vistas of 'natural landscape'. To be Natural was paradoxically an artificial ideal, an attempt to create a harmonious landscape painting out of real life. If real life did not fit into the landscape, real life was the loser – unsightly objects such as poorly spaced trees, hedges or even labourers' cottages were removed to enhance the 'naturalness' of the view. Flowers and signs of deliberate cultivation had to be hidden.

The leading theorist of this style of gardening was William Kent who 'leaped the fence and saw that all nature was a garden'. His ideas were taken up by a head gardener called 'Capability' Brown, who made his name by creating an artificial lake to improve the natural landscape for the Duke of Grafton in Northamptonshire. In retrospect, Brown is credited with destroying more of England's gardening heritage than any other individual. Brown was supposed to have turned down a job in Ireland because he 'hadn't finished England yet'. Eleanor Sinclair Rohde, a gardening historian, commented in 1932:

Why our flower-loving nation tolerated such vandalism it is hard to understand. So far from making or attempting to improve gardens the landscape 'gardeners' destroyed them, substituting fields and lawns and 'natural' lakes and streams.

The large-scale earthworks necessary to create a 'natural landscape' ruled out the involvement of women and they almost disappear as objects of gardening literature whilst 'Capability' Brown was on the rampage. But fashion spreads unevenly; there are always contradictory or unrelated currents and ideas running alongside one another. Gilbert White, at Selborne, Hampshire, still had his weeding woman. He wrote to his niece in 1778:

> I am now going to retain my weeding woman for the summer. This is the person that Thomas [the gardener and a self-declared misogynist] says he likes as well as a man: and indeed excepting that she wears petticoats, and now and then has a child, you'd think her a man. To the care and abilities of this lady I shall entrust my garden.

Other than landscape gardening, the most important development of the eighteenth century was the system of plant classification introduced by Carl Linnaeus in 1753 which made it possible to describe and group plants more rigorously. Philip Miller was rude to the young Linnaeus when he visited Chelsea Physic Garden. 'This botanist doesn't know a single plant,' he is supposed to have said. (Fortunately for his own reputation, Miller changed his mind.)

Linnaean classification is based on the sexual functions of plants. All flowering plants are grouped according to the male organs, the stamens of the flower. They are then subgrouped according to female organs, the style or stigma. Linnaeus himself coyly personified the plants; he described the group Diandra as 'two husbands in the same marriage', and Polyandria as 'twenty males or more in the same bed with the female'. Erasmus Darwin, the grandfather of Charles, respected the simplicity of the Linnaean system but cruelly parodied the metaphor. Turmeric (*Curcuma*) for instance has one fertile stamen, and four sterile stamens which Linnaeus called 'eunuchs'. This is one stanza of Darwin's verse.

Elizabeth Blackwell's illustration of a mandrake root from her book *A Curious Herbal*. She drew the picture at Chelsea Physic Garden.

Woo'd with long care, Curcuma cold and shy
Meets her fond husband with averted eye:
Four beardless youths the obdurate beauty move
With soft attentions of Platonic love.

Darwin's scandalous verses had their repercussions on gardening texts. Whilst plant forms were interesting, women gardeners had misgivings about acknowledging the sexuality of plants. Henrietta Moriarty, in her *Fifty Plates of Greenhouse Plants* (1803), said in the introduction, 'This work is intended for those who take a delight in plants but have not the advantage of a gardener who understands them.' She goes on to argue that natural history was important but it could be taken too far. Her book was:

> . . . entirely free from these ingenious speculations and allusions, which, however suited to the physiologist, are dangerous to the young and ignorant: for this reason I have taken as little notice as possible of the system of the immortal Linnaeus . . . nay I have not once named the fanciful Dr Darwin.

This book was one of a new genre, aimed at the emerging boarding school market. Well-brought-up girls were sent away to school for a very basic grounding in literacy, topped up by needlework, raised pastry-making, dancing, drawing and botany. Botany was thought to aid the 'health of the body and cheerfulness of disposition by presenting an inducement to take air

Rosa provencialis, one of the illustrations from Mary Lawrence's book *A Collection of Roses from Nature* published in 1799.

and exercise'. The ingredients of these new books – *The British Garden* by Charlotte Murray (1799), *A Collection of Roses from Nature* by Miss Mary Lawrence (1799), *An Introduction to Botany* by Priscilla Wakefield (1796), and several others – were botanical drawing, with a little botanical information, interspersed with homilies about behaviour. The ratios varied according to the author. Charlotte Murray was relatively restrained.

> The ardent and active powers of the imagination are constantly gratified by the acquisition of knowledge, and it is a delight to roam in the flowery paths of vegetable luxuriance.

The most famous instruction book of all, *Elementary Letters on Botany to a Lady* was by Jean-Jacques Rousseau, later illustrated by Pierre-Joseph Redouté. Rousseau wrote a series of letters on botany to a four-year-old girl (who was either very precocious or who had a mother with an eye for posterity). However, that story belongs to Redouté, who is discussed in a later chapter.

Over the next few decades botany separated out again from gardening, although the homilies remained. By 1827 Maria E. Jackson was offering her *Florist's Manual* or *Hints for the Construction of a Gay Flower Garden*. She writes for women, whom she addresses as 'sister-florists' and 'sister-gardeners'. She assumes that 'a Flower-Garden is now become a necessary appendage to every fashionable residence', and that 'the common' or 'Mingled Flower-Garden' should be situated so as to form 'an ornamental appendage to the house'. Her book has sections on how to keep the garden gay with 'enamelled borders'; on the treatment and growth of bulbous plants; and hints on avoiding the depredations of snails (slices of turnip scattered upon the borders). She gives advice on layout:

> . . . it is essential that the separate parts should, in their appearance constitute a WHOLE; and that this appearance is more easily affected if the borders are *straight.*

Miss Jackson may have been a keen gardener, but she was also a windbag.

> Having, from early childhood to advanced age, possessed, I may almost say, a hereditary liking for this lovely order of creation, and having, from the subject, in all its branches, derived the most interesting amusement of my youth, I am solicitous to render to my sister-florists, partakers of my pleasures, so far at least, as by laying before them a few hints, the result of experience, I may enable them so methodically to arrange and blend the colours of their flowers, that through most part of the spring and summer months they may procure a succession of enamelled borders, which without the knowledge of the tints afforded by each season cannot be made to exhibit half the charms that a flower garden well conducted, has the capacity of presenting to the view.

The giant of early nineteenth-century gardening is John Loudon, and his *Encyclopedia of Gardening*, published in 1822 and reprinted throughout the century, is a magisterial reference book. He was the founder and editor of a number of gardening magazines, and he poured out an incessant stream of advice in books and articles on gardening techniques, garden design, the education of gardeners, and the need for public parks and well-kept cemeteries. His characteristic tone was described by the garden writer Ray Desmond as 'a Calvinistic zeal wedded to a pontifical manner'.

In 1831 he married Jane Wells. She was a science-fiction writer, and he had noticed a review of her work *The Mummy* and wrote to her. She became his devoted companion, and most ardent supporter. In a biographical note written after his death, she describes how they used to work together closely.

> The labour that attended this work [a new encyclopedia] was immense; for several months he and I used to sit up the greater part of every night, never having more than four hours sleep, and drinking strong coffee to keep ourselves awake.

One of Loudon's rivals, the intemperate editor of the *Gardener's Gazette*, George Glenny, considered Jane Loudon exacerbated all her husband's worst faults. In a vituperative editorial he wrote,

> We assure Mr Loudon that his old woman is a mischievious bedlam . . . We hate old women at the best of times, but a lying old woman is abominable and the sooner Loudon shakes the hag off the better.

Not surprisingly, Glenny was eventually sacked, although not because of this comment. Jane Loudon went on from strength to strength. She wrote a bestseller, *Instruction in Gardening for Ladies*, which was praised by the American writer Elizabeth Lawrence, over a century later, for offering the best advice about growing bulbs she had ever read. For a year in 1840 Jane ran a woman's magazine, *The Ladies' Magazine of Gardening*, but the strain of this and nursing her ailing workaholic husband must have been considerable.

The format of the *Ladies' Magazine* followed that of her husband's *Gardener's Magazine*. There was a review of new plants displayed at the horticultural shows with engravings and colour plates; a floral calendar which gave month by month gardening advice, including indoor gardening; articles about garden furniture and garden implements ('one of the most teasing things that a lady can meet with in the cultivation of her plants is a badly made watering pot'); a wild-life slot mainly about birds, but on one occasion about a pet dog. She also visited many gardens, and commented on their design and upkeep. There was a correspondence column.

> An invalid lady living in a remote part of the country has long devoted herself to the cultivation of flowers. A great source of amusement has been to bring wild flowers into the garden where they grow luxuriantly but all the care and attention bestowed on them have not succeeded in making any

of them double . . . is there any truth in the old saying that by planting a primrose with the head downwards it will change the colour of the flower?

Jane tactfully replied that 'it was a popular error handed down through the centuries but never tested'.

John Loudon died in 1843 but Jane continued writing. Her *Ladies' Companion to the Flower-Garden* sold more than 20,000 copies and her advice, influenced by her husband's ideas, was widely followed. She believed in the 'gardenesque', that is in gardens which were designed to show off the artistry of the gardener.

Flower gardens are of two kinds: those that are called natural and which are planted without any regard to regularity; and those that are called geometric and which consist of beds forming some definite figure.

For her, the English style in gardening was essentially a matter of regularity and neatness. She put forward views about the order and size of flower beds – she preferred circular beds.

> When a flower garden is laid out in a regular figure there can only be one or two points of view from which it can be seen to best advantage . . . this can never be the case . . . if they are either ovals or circles.

Like her husband, she adopted theories of colour arrangement, believing that primary colours should be placed next to compound colours. Each circular bed should have its own colour theme, either of one colour, or of one colour and its complementary colour. Careful attention should be paid to the height of plants. 'The centre bed alone may have the taller plants.'

FAR LEFT
The frontispiece of Maria Jackson's book *The Florist's Manual*. She described a garden as 'an ornamental appendage to the home' and stressed the desirability of neatly edged 'enamelled borders'.

LEFT
Jane Loudon, early science-fiction writer, devoted wife, nurse and amanuensis of Victorian garden writer John Loudon, and best-selling author of gardening books for women.

It was acknowledged that not everyone would have the space for circular beds. In this case they could honour Linnaeus and their garden could display 'a miniature representation of the Natural System of Botany – all the ranunculus, the fumitory and poppies, the cruciferous plants' grouped together.

Jane also recommended garden furniture, rustic seats, bowers, moss houses with thatched or shingled roofs and pebbled floors, rockwork, ornamented pots – the garden equivalent of an over-furnished Victorian drawing room.

Jane Loudon's last book was called *The Ladies' Country Companion* and was written in the form of a series of letters to a lady called Annie, living in the country. It gives advice about setting up the house as well as the garden and how to persuade tactfully an obstinate husband to make changes. One letter comments on the charitable role well-to-do country ladies were supposed to undertake. She said it was important to assist the poor, but on no account should Annie embroider baby clothes:

> . . . the feelings of the poor are often hurt by having dictated to them what they are to wear . . . they are apt to look upon the clothes thus given them . . . almost as a badge of slavery which they are compelled to wear to please their patrons, but of which they hate the very sight.

This switch by women writers from gardening advice to other domestic or religious advice was quite common. Victorian women, as a female columnist in the magazine *The Cottage Gardener* pointed out in 1848, may have had a legitimate interest in gardens but they were also expected to be guardians of morality.

> Woman has much in her power. Wives and mothers have great duties to perform; they are the mainsprings of the moral world and even among their fragrant flowers they may cull instruction and impart lessons of wisdom.

One of the most prolific of Victorian writers was a lady called Anne Pratt whose life spanned the century. She was 20 when she wrote her first gardening book *Flowers and Their Associations* in 1826. The book for which she was best known, *Flowering Plants, Grasses, Sedges and Ferns of Great Britain*, was a standard, four-volume reference book which was constantly reprinted in Britain and in the U.S.A. It offered an illustration and a description of each plant, and some historical background about its cultivation. It was handy and easy to read, and free of moralizing. However, she also wrote some excruciating religious tracts. In a little book called *Nature's Wonders*, or *God's Care Over All His Works*, published in 1850, she told the story of a little boy called Alexander.

'Now, dear Mamma', said the little boy one bright morning, 'long winter seems really gone. Look how the sun shines and the ground is quite dry; may we not go into the woods for some striped snail-shells for my grotto? Can you not spare the time to put away your work and walk with me this lovely weather?'
[His mother agrees.] 'Doubtless I shall work all the more industriously after the exercise and you will learn better for having your mind refreshed by open air'.

No wonder that the *Journal of Botany* published only a two-line obituary of her in 1893. 'She was the author of a large number of popular and in the main accurate books about plants, chiefly British ones.'

The Victorian age was the great age of gardening. Gardening magazines were started one after the other. As Brent Elliott pointed out in his scholarly book *Victorian Gardens*, inventions included wrought-iron glazing bars and sheet glass for glasshouses, linseed oil putty, Portland cement for rockeries, and the Wardian case for transporting plants from abroad, and – possibly the most important – the lawn-mower! The abolition of glass tax in 1845 put greenhouse gardening and propagation of plants within reach of many. The railways made transport of plants and people to and from nurseries and gardens much easier.

These innovations led to a flourishing of horticultural science and experimentation with the hardiness of plants, forcing, soil sterilization, fertilizers, pruning and training, and above all with plant breeding. New colourful plants were introduced from the colonies and tropics, raised under glass, and planted out as annuals.

The Victorian age was also the age of the professional gardener. From Joseph Paxton onwards, they dominate Victorian gardening literature, editing the influential magazines, becoming the arbiters of garden taste. In one famous case a head gardener sued his lady employer for libel – she had accused him of laziness – and won.

There were often difficulties between the lady owners and gardeners. Louisa Johnson in *Every Lady her Own Flower Gardener* (1837) was persuaded to write her book by

> . . . many of my companions . . . [for] the amusement of floriculture has become the dominant passion of the ladies of Great Britain: 'We require' they said 'a work small in compass which will enable us to become our own gardener: we wish to know every thing *ourselves*'.

She starts off with what to wear.

> Every lady should be furnished with a gardening apron, composed of stout Holland, with ample pockets to contain her pruning knife, a small stout hammer, a ball of string, and a few nails and snippings of cloth. Have nothing to do with scissors . . .

Her gardening advice was not good. She recommended Michaelmas daisies as a plant for January, and fed bulbs with salt. She valued tidiness.

> I cannot lay too great stress upon the neatness in which a lady's garden should be kept. If it is not beautifully neat, it is nothing.

Her book touched an audience, sold well and ran to seven editions. This persuaded her to have another go. In *Every Lady's Guide to her Own Greenhouse* (1851) she gets into her stride. A lady must

> . . . if she has any regard to her own comfort obtain a man who does not know too much . . . and [does] not act on his own opinion; for it is unpleasant to be subject to the invisible sneers of a man who considers you wrong.

The greenhouse book is more knowledgeable and offers sound advice on technical subjects such as boiler maintenance, piping systems and watering devices, with diagrams. Men are definitely the enemy.

> I declare I know ladies who submit to black looks, impertinent remarks, rude sneers, and other uncouth behaviour in a manner I would not submit to even from my husband.

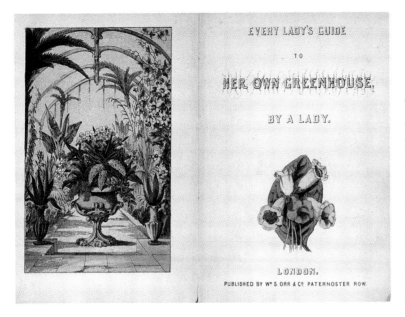

The frontispiece to *Every Lady's Guide to her Own Greenhouse*, by Louisa Johnson, who thought women perfectly capable of mastering the principles of heating and plumbing necessary in a Victorian greenhouse.

Louisa's feelings are echoed by 'Rosa', the female columnist of the *Cottage Gardener*, although Rosa is more sentimental.

> A flower garden is a great resource to a lady. We have, in our rather limited sphere, a good deal to suffer, and a good deal to make the best of, and, in each case, our minds seem mollified by the sight and smell of our gay and fragrant parterres.

However, a few months later Rosa writes more indignantly

> A lady with a good gardener begins cheerfully at first, but in a year or two it is all over. She walks round the glowing borders but her interest is gone. To enjoy your garden thoroughly you must say with Queen Elizabeth 'I will have but one mistress here and no master'.

All the gardening magazines made some effort to interest lady readers and to include items purporting to be of interest to them. The *Gardener's Chronicle*, for instance, printed an article by a gardener called Alex Forsyth about ladies for whom he had worked. These included the Duchess of Northumberland who was on such intimate terms with her garden that 'if a snail had eaten a flower in the night, the Duchess would have missed it from its place in the morning and bewailed it'. Mr Forsyth concluded that 'where man and wife differ in their ideas as to which way their garden is to be managed, let them separate and have each a garden of their own, each taking his or her solitary way'. The *Gardener's Chronicle*, for some inexplicable reason, also kept up a long-running correspondence in the 1860s on poultry keeping for ladies. The short lived *Villa Gardener*, founded in 1870, still had Louisa Johnson in mind when it declared in an advertisement:

> It being unquestionable that it is on the ladies of the Household that the general direction of the labour of a Flower Garden falls . . . it will be the particular study of the Conductors, by imparting their experience on the best mode of management, to make 'Every Lady her Own Flower Gardener'.

The first edition of the *Cottage Gardener*, in 1848, carried this extraordinary obituary.

> The late Mrs Davis Gilbert of Eastbourne was ever a warm and consistent friend of cottage gardens . . . she sought to accomplish [home comforts] by a variety of excellent and successful efforts, such as the more extensive introduction of deeper digging or forking . . . by the collection, as a manure, of cottage sewage.

But even the *Cottage Gardener*, which later changed its name to the *The Journal of Horticulture, Cottage Gardener and Country Gentlemen*, was not about cottage gardens, except in making suggestions about how the philanthropic middle classes – like Mrs Davis Gilbert – could help cottagers improve their hygiene. Most recorded history is about the upper and middle classes, about the minority rather than the majority. In the new Victorian cities, the poverty and long factory hours left no time or money for gardening, except an occasional allotment.

Rural poverty was equally grinding, although accounts exist of more well-to-do farming households. Mary Mitford, in *Our Village* (1832), describes how Hannah Bint, from Miles Cross Farm near Reading, loved her flower garden.

> She was a real genuine florist and adored oddities that importation and crossing had produced rather than the simple beauty of natural flowers. This was the only flaw in an otherwise perfect character.

Mary Mitford, who lived in genteel rural poverty, was no mean gardener herself. She raised chrysanthemums and dahlias and in a letter dated 1845 she writes, 'One of my seedlings is so fine that we have sold it for £20, the highest price given for a dahlia this year'. This profit paid her heating bills for a year. She was less lucky with her prize geraniums (of which she had 300 varieties): on one occasion the cat trod on them; on another they were stolen; and on yet another the stove chimney smoked and poisoned them.

She had many visitors. 'I was befraddled by the eternal visitors who make this cottage during the summer and autumn months a sort of tea-garden.'

She supplied the local nurseryman with plants, and in 1854, just before she died, she was writing to John Ruskin about plants for picking. 'By far the most gorgeous flower-jar that I ever made was the double white narcissus studded with choice ranunculus, not hanging loose, but tightly packed together.'

Miss Mitford was not bothered with the fashionable styles of gardening, and preferred 'humble plants' (apart from geraniums and dahlias). But fashion itself was changing. Towards the end of the century there was another swing of style, away from geometric beds, bedding out and the use of brightly coloured tender annuals, and the reliance on the expertise of head gardeners. The protagonist of the 'new' movement was William Robinson, an ex-head gardener and editor of a gardening magazine. His book *The Wild Garden* (1870) promoted a style of gardening which was not really wild but relied heavily on perennial herbaceous and native plants. His own garden at Gravetye Manor, West Sussex, was extremely well kept, as Vita Sackville-West noticed when as a young woman she was taken to see it. The 90-year-old Robinson drove her round in a motorized mower at such a fast pace and at such precarious angles that, as she noted in her memoir of him, she was terrified.

Robinson's views were ripe for the time. One of his supporters was Mrs Earle, another woman in the tradition of Victorian lady writers, who combined gardening notes with cookery recipes (in which brown sauce predominated), and hints about how to bring up girls. Mrs Earle wrote her first book *Pot-Pourri from a Surrey Garden* in 1897 at the age of 61, and it was an instant best-seller.

Through her eyes we see glimpses of the gardening preoccupations of the late Victorian era. Mrs Earle did not agree wholeheartedly with Robinson

A contemporary photograph of Gravetye Manor, once the garden of William Robinson, the quarrelsome but gifted gardener and journalist, who sounded the 'death-note' of Victorian bedding. He advocated perennials, and a more informal use of plants.

Kindly, well-connected Mrs Earle, disciple of William Robinson, and friend of Gertrude Jekyll – whom she described as an ambitious and enthusiastic amateur. She wrote best-selling homely books, giving gardening advice interspersed with household hints.

about clearing out the gardenesque furniture – she still favoured an occasional statue or sundial – but she did agree about the horrors of bedding schemes. She was preoccupied with flowers for the house, especially in winter, and there is much discussion about forcing, stovehouse plants, the effects of cutting back shrubs in order to have flowering branches indoors for decoration – she insists almost all shrubs benefit from very heavy pruning. She is concerned with feeding plants – properly 'manuring, chalking, mulching'. She grows quantities of vegetables, and relishes fresh vegetables for the house. She thinks that 'wild gardens' require 'endless care' in order to look beautiful. She goes garden visiting and comments that whilst gardens in the south have changed 'by the reintroducing of old fashioned flowers and the old methods of cultivating them', those in the north are much slower to change.

Apparently changes work slower in the North than around London. I wonder why this is? . . . One would have thought that the fashion which has so influenced us would have influenced them. I saw in many places long borders planted with rows of red, violet, white, yellow and purple . . . Why they ever came in and why they have lasted so long it is difficult to understand. The gardens of rich and poor, big house and villa were planted on the same system – perennials in lines, annuals in lines, Mignonette in lines; and where long lines were not possible, the planting was in rows around the shrubbery, which is, I think, the ugliest thing I know.

For small gardens, Mrs Earle recommends avoiding 'coarse-growing shrubs':

I should not allow anything coarser-growing than the green and variegated Box, the golden Privet, Bay Tree (which can be constantly cut back), Daturas, *Viburnum plicatum*, Irish Yews, Cotoneaster grown as a bush, *Choisya ternata*, Berberises, *Buddleia globosa* . . .

From contemporary accounts, Mrs Earle was a pleasant, tolerant and hospitable woman, rooted in her generation but nevertheless sympathetic to the young, and somewhat radical in her political views:

To me some few flowers seem vulgar, partly from association and partly from the unsympathetic harshness of their tint. But surely in gardening, as in all else in life, the broadest view is best, and the wisest attempt is to please as many as we can. The taste of the ignorant and the critical taste of the cultivated can never be the same on any subject, but both are better than indifference and no taste at all . . . All tastes are respectable, though we may each of us find it difficult to admire the taste of another.

Women have been a target audience for gardening advice through the centuries. Their influence was continually acknowledged even if their intelligence was held in doubt. But they were much more than recipients of advice. They bred and exhibited plants. They collected them from remote places whilst accompanying their husbands on colonial adventures, or sometimes even on their own. They drew plants for the great botanical collections. They were botanists contributing to local surveys. As the next chapter shows, they created some very remarkable gardens. But only at the end of the nineteenth century were they free enough truly to make their mark.

CHAPTER TWO

WEALTH AND OBSESSIONS

The Royal Horticultural Society was founded as the Horticultural Society of London in 1804. It was, John Loudon thundered, no more than an exclusive gentlemen's club. New members were only admitted through election, and women were not admitted at all. Women were first considered for membership in the 1820s because it was thought they might have advantages as fund-raisers. The Society set up a committee of 24 lady patrons, of whom 20 were titled ladies, to organize its public fund-raising breakfast in 1827. The public breakfast was attended by 2843 persons of standing. The Society's minutes read:

> . . . it was allowed by all parties that such an assemblage of women of beauty, fashion and rank, had never before been seen in a garden.

The event was a financial success but was heavily criticized for being a fashion show rather than a horticultural event. The Society held another breakfast in 1828, this time restricted to Fellows and their wives. The problems about exclusivity and horticultural expertise remained but, by June 1830, the pressure to admit women had become irresistible. The Countess of Radnor (who had the same privilege as a peer and had no need for a ballot), Mrs Holland, Mrs Marryat, Mrs Thornton and Mrs Louisa Collier were elected

A stone urn framed by *Rosa* 'Nathalie Nypels'
at Tintinhull in Somerset.

as members. A month later the Countess of Guildford and the Countess of Morton were admitted and, shortly afterwards, Mrs Louisa Lawrence.

Two of these women at least, Mrs Marryat and Mrs Lawrence, had famous gardens. Mrs Lawrence had a garden at Draycott Park in Ealing, west London, where she employed six men and two women (for weeding and collecting dead leaves) and had regular displays of verbenas, *Salvia patens*, and fuchsias. She is recorded as having over 3000 varieties of plants, and specialized in pelargoniums and orchids. Unkind gossip suggested that she denuded several tropical forests of their original specimens in her enthusiasm to acquire new rare orchids. Jane Loudon praised her orchid house 'beautifully arranged' and also her collection of cape heaths: 'For my own part I was never very fond

ABOVE
An engraving of Mrs Lawrence's picturesque villa garden.

RIGHT
Mrs Marryat's palatial planthouses where she cultivated her 'exotics'.

of heaths, but the sight of Mrs Lawrence's heathery has quite converted me.' By 1838 Mrs Lawrence had won over 53 prizes for her plants at the Horticultural Shows, including the coveted Knightian medal.

Mrs Marryat of Wimbledon, south London, was the first female recipient of plants on the Society's distribution list. Like Mrs Lawrence she won prizes regularly at the Society Shows, amongst other things for her yellow azaleas and her strawberries. She was famous for the 'exotics' she cultivated in her palatial greenhouse range.

These ladies belonged to the very highest society. Mrs Lawrence was a well-known hostess; her afternoon parties were attended by the Queen and Prince Consort, and European royalty. The engraving below of Mrs Marryat's

EXHIBITION EXTRAORDINARY in the HORTICULTURAL ROOM.

A cartoon by Cruikshank ridiculing a meeting of the Horticultural Society.

garden gives some idea of the scale of her fortune and influence.

All the women whose gardens were recorded in any detail before the twentieth century belong to the upper-classes, since no one else had the leisure or income to garden on such a magnificent scale, nor the confidence or status to entertain the eminent gardening writers of their day who might publicize or record their gardens for posterity. But even though they were drawn from a narrow range of society, there were a surprising number of them. The Duchess of Beaufort was admired by many of her contemporaries, and cited by the Society of Gardeners in 1732 for her collection of exotic plants at Badminton in Avon. Some fifty years earlier in 1685, in his book *Upon the Garden of Epicurus,* Sir William Temple was praising the Duchess of Bedford for her garden at Moor Park, Hertfordshire, which he described as a garden constructed 'with very great care, excellent contrivance and much cost'.

Great parlours open into the middle of a terrace gravel walk that lies even within it, and which may be, as I remember, about 300 paces long and broad proportion; the border set with standard laurels, and at large distances, which have the beauty of orange trees and out of flower fruit: from this walk are three descents by many stone steps, in the middle and at each end, into a very large parterre.

A youthful portrait of the Duchess of Portland, patroness of the arts and sciences, correspondent of Rousseau, and a keen botanist and gardener.

There were further gravel walks, two summer houses, one vine covered cloister, and one with myrtles 'and other greens'. There was also a grotto 'and several quarters of a wilderness which is very shady'. The Duchess had several gardens but Moor Park was the best known, and Sir William thought it would serve, 'for a pattern to the best gardens of our manners, and that are most proper for our country and climate'.

Most famous of all for her gardening activities was the Duchess of Portland. Margaret Cavendish Bentinck gardened for over 50 years at Bulstrode. She had literary and artistic connections as well as botanic connections; she was a friend of David Garrick, James Boswell and Joshua Reynolds, as well as of Joseph Banks and Sir Hans Soane. She sponsored plant hunting expeditions abroad, and she was a correspondent of Jean-Jacques Rousseau, with whom she went hiking in the Peak District to look for plants. She had different types of gardens at Bulstrode: an ancient garden, an American garden, a flower garden, a botanic garden, a kitchen garden, a shrubbery and a parterre. She was scientifically minded – she left a collection of exercise books filled with accurate descriptions of plants and fungi, and notes about plants she had purchased. She had an outstanding collection of roses, one of which, the Portland rose, is named after her, although its provenance is not entirely clear.

By the time Jane Loudon was writing in the mid-nineteenth century, new money had made its mark and it was the well-to-do middle classes whom she visited. One of the gardens she most admired was that of Lady Broughton. This 'villa' garden at Hoole House, Chester, had 27 circular raised flower beds with wire baskets on each, in an area 60 yards long by 34 yards wide. As well as filling the circular beds with brightly coloured annuals, Lady Broughton was an alpine enthusiast. She had 'the most remarkable and best executed rock garden in existence'. There was a scale model of the Alps, with white granite to represent snow, and a variety of alpine flora which it had taken her eight years to establish. Judging from the number of engravings of this garden it was widely known and admired, and a talking point of gardening magazines.

Jane Loudon also wrote about lesser luminaries: Mrs Wilkie from Uddingstone in Lanarkshire, 'a lady gardener whose beautiful flower-garden showed ample proof of the care and attention lavished upon it'; and Lady Mary Stanley whose 'flower beds on the lawn were all in circles'. She must have also visited or known of Lady Middleton, whose garden at Shrubland Park near Ipswich in Suffolk was written up in the *Gardener's Chronicle* in 1856.

> Each border is occupied with three continuous lines of colour extending their whole length. The first on each side of the walk is blue; the second yellow; and the third on one side is scarlet and on the other white. The following plants are employed on the one side: *Nemophila insignis* for blue; *Calceolaria rugosa* for yellow, and the Frogmore geranium for scarlet.

Lady Middleton and her head gardener Donald Beaton represented the apotheosis of Victorian gardening. After this climax of floral display, garden planting schemes became quieter again. One of the most influential gardeners of the 1860s and 1870s was Frances Hope of Wardie House in Edinburgh. She was the spinster daughter of a well-to-do banking family which had made money in railway speculation, although from her frequent strictures on economy in the garden, it is hard to tell she is wealthy. The *Gardener's Chronicle* set aside its editorial of May 1880 for her obituary.

> Her plants were her pets, but in cherishing them she employed discrimination and tact amounting almost to genius. Her taste in selecting plants was only equalled by her skill in cultivating them . . . Miss Hope was, to

a large extent her own gardener. That goes without saying. To many gardeners the garden is everything, the plants are mere accessories. This was not Miss Hope's way of viewing things; for her the garden existed for the plants, not the plants for the garden.

The editorial praises fulsomely her collection of bulbs and hellebores, her search for and rescue of 'many fine old plants, now lost and neglected', and her generosity in sharing her findings with other amateurs. She was exceptionally hard working:

> Her garden was the great interest of her life. She was up early and at work late in it – working as hard as her men and doing everything much better than they. She spared no pains to add to her collection, and had visited every garden of importance in England and Scotland.

After her death her niece collected and edited the notes and letters she had written for various gardening magazines and published them under the title *Notes and Thoughts on Gardens and Woodlands*. Miss Hope extolled the virtues of careful observation. Writing about her beloved hellebores, she says:

> I advise you above all to see plants at all their ages, to follow their growth, to describe them in detail; in one word to live with them more than with books . . . one can never know too much about a plant; one can never know all there is to be learnt.

She firmly believed in self-improvement, and her asides about it are dotted through her writing: 'There is no doubt one's own ignorance is the main cause of one's want of success,' and, 'I do not see why we should encourage growth and progress in our plants, and get mentally contracted and stunted ourselves.'

She had advanced views on bedding:

> When it is remembered that a winter garden must last for seven months and on the other hand that the summer display is at most four months, there is no question as to which is the more important of the two . . . for fourteen years our 'modern flower garden' has not been bare . . . nor has it once been filled on the deplorable makeshift plan of cut branches merely stuck in the ground.

LEFT

The miniature mountain range at Hoole House in Cheshire, home of
Lady Broughton. She was a passionate alpine gardener and
constructed a model of the Alps covered with white granite chippings
to represent snow. Her garden, which also included 27 circular
raised flower beds, was one of the most widely praised
early-Victorian gardens.

BELOW

Lady Middleton's garden, Shrubland. The blue, yellow and scarlet
bedding schemes were widely known and admired, although there
was some dispute between her and her equally famous head
gardener, Donald Beaton, as to who should have most credit
for the work.

In her garden, which was close to the sea, relatively unsheltered and with poor light soil, she had 35 beds, including a ribbon border 86 feet long, which relied heavily on sedums, sempervivums and rosemaries (which were also used in nosegays for the blind), and circular beds varying from a circle 13 feet in diameter, to the smallest of five and a half feet in diameter. In the 1860s, each of the circular beds had a centre of evergreens, then a ring of colour and an edging of variegation, with early bulbs. The colour was mainly produced by brassicas or sea-kale:

> By the use of them you obtain every shade from the darkest purple of the Siberian to a vivid magenta, mauve and rose . . . also pure yellow and white.

This use of brassicas was also economical. Miss Hope no longer used tender shrubs which were too delicate or too difficult to lift and move out the beds for winter: 'It was the first and last experiment on a grand scale. A few shillings, *not* yearly, now suffice.'

By 1875 she had modified her views slightly:

> Bed no. 2 has *Campanula carpatica* (blue) with broad edgings of the yellow *Oenothera missouriensis*. No. 13 has *Yucca gloriosa* set in a groundwork of dark blue *Ajuga purpurescens*, dotted with *Sedum spectabile*.

A hanging-basket design by Miss Frances Hope, a highly respected late-Victorian gardener. She liked brown varnished wickerwork, and houseleeks.

She also had vigorous opinions on hanging baskets. She was bored with ferns and trailing geraniums, and favoured houseleeks stuck on the outside of the basket. She liked brown varnished wickerwork.

> After trying many plans, we have found nothing so good as baskets of close texture, painted and varnished a warm brown, a colour which detracts from nothing and harmonizes with everything.

Miss Hope was the most famous and influential woman gardener in the 1860s and 1870s. Another well-known woman gardener, slightly later, was the Hon. Evelyn Vere Boyle, who also wrote notes for gardening magazines, and several books. Her style is not so crisp and authoritative as that of Miss Hope, and her books are now almost unreadable. But her garden at Huntercombe in Buckinghamshire was very well known and visited. It showed how styles were changing from the Victorian use of bedding plants to subdivided gardens using perennial herbaceous plants.

> There are now close-trimmed Yew hedges, some of the first planted being 8ft 6 high and near 3 ft through . . . the borders are filled with dearest old-fashioned plants.

Annuals are still being used for colour in parts of the garden, and self-seeding is allowed.

> The entrance court is bright with Nicotiana, Scarlet Pelargoniums, zinnias, double white petunia and blue lobelias. Torch plants [*tritonia*] are alight in all the edges of distant shrubberies. There are Japan Anemones and Oenothera everywhere. The sweet-pea hedge by the tennis court is out again in bloom. Marigolds take care of themselves. They keep going off and coming on again . . . Golden rod is plentiful and useful and I like it for the sake of old remembrance.

In 1897 the Victoria Medal of Honour, the highest award of the Royal Horticultural Society, was inaugurated and given for the first time to two women together, Gertrude Jekyll and Ellen Willmott. The story of Gertrude Jekyll belongs to another chapter. Ellen Willmott truly characterizes this chapter's theme of wealth and obsession. She spent her vast fortune on the

RIGHT
Ellen Willmott – rich, ambitious and arrogant – who created a fabulous garden at Warley Place in Essex. She was an internationally renowned plantswoman and holder of the Royal Horticultural Society's Victoria Medal of Honour but she died in penury, unable to pay her rates.

BELOW
The annual photograph of the garden staff at Warley Place, taken by Miss Willmott. The gardeners wore a uniform of straw boaters with green ribbons, navy-blue aprons and knitted green silk ties. In her heyday, Ellen Willmott employed 104 gardeners.

most famous and beautiful garden of her generation at Warley Place in Essex and died bankrupt with her garden in ruins.

It is difficult now to appreciate Ellen Willmott's importance but for a time she was the most respected, and internationally revered, British gardener. Gertrude Jekyll referred to her as 'the greatest of living gardeners'. She was only 38 when she was awarded the Medal. She first became known as a daffodil grower and hybridizer. She was a member of the R.H.S. Narcissus Committee, whose members included the nurseryman Amos Perry, and Henry de Vilmorin, the noted French horticulturalist, and she impressed them greatly with her enthusiasm, knowledge and intelligence.

Her correspondents and visitors came from all over the world. She was thought to be unrivalled as a cultivator of difficult plants. She was growing several New Zealand plants and shrubs long before their general introduction. She contributed financially to plant hunting expeditions, and was the first to raise some of Ernest Wilson's seeds from China. She was tireless in finding the right condition for seeds, tending plants, making skilled observation of their progress, and administering quick first aid when necessary. She was noted for her primula hybrids and her roses. In her heyday she had over 100,000 varieties of plants at Warley Place, many of them her own cultivars. She won many awards of merit from the R.H.S. for her new introductions.

She employed a staff of 104 gardeners to look after her 55 acres of garden. She photographed them annually in their uniforms of boaters in natural straw with green ribbons, navy-blue aprons and knitted green silk ties. She had two other gardens, one in France and one in Italy, and was as much a martinet with her staff there as in Warley Place. She printed postcards with the address of each of her homes, so her head gardeners could communicate constantly with her.

She came of a gardening family – both her mother and her sister Rose were keen gardeners. Her alpine garden began as a present from her mother for her twenty-first birthday. She kept detailed notes of all her plants, eagle-eyed for good form and new varieties; each variety was numbered, and new trials were meticulously recorded. She was an accomplished photographer, developing her own film, and made a photographic record of the garden, as well as the gardeners who cultivated it. She had her own printing press for the seed lists. (She also had a microscope, a telescope, expensive wood-turning equipment and metal working tools, and a very valuable collection of musical instruments.)

Her skill and investment as a gardener were outstanding. In the words of George Wilson from Wisley, 'it seems to me that your garden is the happiest combination of alpine, herbaceous and florist flowers that I have ever seen'.

Although no expense was too great for her garden, Ellen Willmott was arrogant and dictatorial and became more so with age. Her biographer, Audrey le Lievre, says,

Lilium × *testaceum*, the hybrid of *Lilium candidum* and *Lilium chalcedonicum*, popularly known as the Nankeen lily, growing luxuriantly when Warley Place was in its prime.

There must have come a time when, almost without knowing it she reached the point where she could no longer be bothered to conceal the fact that she was more knowledgeable, quick-witted, and intelligent than most of the men she knew.

Ellen Willmott was reputed to have said to a friend – in front of a pink rose – 'That is Cupid: I knew him not,' and, later, 'As we grow older we find it harder to conceal our faults.' Her argumentative nature (she had various feuds with fellow gardeners) was one fault. (She was so furious with Wilson's wife for trying to dissuade him from going to China that she denounced her as 'a tiresome ignorant woman' and arranged for 'someone to entertain the wife whilst I turn my attention to Wilson'.) Her relentless, obsessive expenditure of time and money on her three gardens was another.

> As you know [she wrote to a friend] my gardens come before anything in life for me and all my time is given up to working in one garden or another, and when it is too dark to see the plants themselves, I read or write about them.

Another damaging fault was her meanness. She gave her gardeners grudging references, and hoarded some of her cultivars. One story describes how she showed some guests around Warley Place

> . . . with great courtesy but also with an eagle eye in case they removed a slip or a head. At the end of the tour, she asked a gardener to take them to a rubbish dump where they might find 'a lot of water buttercup'.

The Director of the Royal Botanic Garden, Kew, Sir William Thistleton-Dyer was cautious about her gifts and wrote in her obituary:

> As gardeners go she was not considered generous and one looked carefully at gift plants for fear they might be fearful spreaders.

Despite her immense fortune, by 1907 she had started to borrow to pay for the gardens. By 1913 she was desperate and had to start selling some of her possessions and renting out part of her properties. But she refused to take financial advice, and her debts increased. She was in danger of being sued for

The garden at Blickling Hall in Norfolk which was redesigned by Norah Lindsay in the 1930s. She removed small fussy beds and kept four big corner beds, filling them with herbaceous plants of graded heights. Each bed has an embroidered border of catmint, mingled with roses.

bankruptcy. Romford Council wanted to prosecute her for non-payment of rates. She had to dismiss many of her gardeners, and gradually the garden deteriorated and the glasshouses were closed. She remained active on her R.H.S. committees: at the age of 75 she was a member of the Floral Committee and the Lily Committee. Her friends and relatives fended off the worst, but she died in penury in 1934. Warley Place was sold to a publican and the garden plundered and left to decay. The *Gardener's Chronicle* noted in her obituary:

> Miss Willmott did nothing by halves. She would by her incisive judgement suggest to the mind a new version of the divine injunction 'Love your enemies' for she undoubtedly got a lot of enjoyment out of them.

In the first half of the twentieth century, three women gardeners stand out, Norah Lindsay, Vita Sackville-West and Phyllis Reiss. Norah Lindsay is an ephemeral figure, and unlike those of the other two, her garden at Sutton Courtenay by the Thames in Berkshire has not survived. She was a romantic lady with a romantic garden. Photographs show her as a stylish Edwardian lady with a wasp waist and a line in large flowery hats. She sometimes has a parasol, with which she was reputed to trace the outlines of the gardens she designed. Only grainy black-and-white photographs survive of her own garden, but they suggest original and extravagant planting.

Writing under the name of Mrs Harry Lindsay (although Harry Lindsay was usually absent), in *Country Life* in 1931, she describes – not modestly – her own garden:

> Some gardens, like some people, have a charm potent to enslave and yet as intangible as dew or vapour. The gardens of the manor of Sutton Courtenay have this shining quality.

She wanted an effect of 'thoughtless abundance'. She liked self-seeding commonplace plants, 'squatters' such as valerian or *Salvia turkestanica* to spread amongst her other plants, within her formal framework of clipped yews.

> Where the flowers themselves have planned the garden, I gracefully retire for they are the guiding intelligences and strike where we fumble. How often

Norah Lindsay in a characteristic Edwardian pose in her garden at Sutton Courtenay. Her garden was original and extravagant, but unfortunately no trace of it remains.

have I perceived a seedling of mullein or anchusa having inlaid itself in the driest and most impossible situation on a wall or in the cracked concrete of a water tank. Here it will successfully wave a rebellious banner, and its cosseted relations, in good soil next door are not half so prosperous or so picturesque.

One gardening writer, Jane Brown, suggested that Norah Lindsay worked very closely with Lawrence Johnston at Hidcote in Gloucestershire, and was its joint creator. (Hidcote was the first garden to be accepted by the National Trust and is now world famous.) Graham Stuart Thomas, the distinguished plantsman, and one-time gardens adviser to the National Trust, disputes this claim, and regards Mrs Muir at next-door Kiftsgate Court as the more influential person in the circle of Gloucestershire gardeners around Johnston. There is more convincing evidence of Norah Lindsay's influence on Blickling Hall in Norfolk (another National Trust property). Her spidery design notes and the garden itself, four big corner beds (two in pink and blue, and mauve and white; two in orange and yellow), still exist.

Part of the difficulty in judging her influence was Norah Lindsay's own socialite personality. It was never quite clear whether she was just visiting her worldly friends at Cliveden, Blickling Hall and other fashionable great houses, and gave friendly advice in passing, or whether she was working as a professional garden designer. On occasions she went to stay as a guest, and then surprised her hosts by submitting hefty bills for her services.

After her death, Sutton Courtenay was sold. Brenda Colvin, the landscape gardener, was asked to redesign the garden. She must have thought it unbearably fussy for she cleared the fabulous long garden at the front of the house and instead put in a gravel drive and lawns.

Norah's daughter, Nancy Lindsay, also left an ambiguous legacy. Some regard her as a great character and gifted gardener, others as a nuisance. Her name occurs again and again in people's reminiscences, sometimes fondly, sometimes dismissively. She inherited her mother's gardening ambitions, and was a rose collector. She had the unfortunate habit of naming old roses she did not recognize with names she invented herself, which caused enormous confusion to later writers about roses.

One of her neighbours, a friend and admirer, describes visiting a restaurant with her, where for some reason she started to describe the sex life of monkeys in her loud, cheerful voice. Gradually everyone in the restaurant put down their knives and forks, and listened, astonished. Nancy took no notice of their reactions and blithely continued. She was an eccentric, she could be extremely good company, generous and immensely knowledgeable, or she could alienate her visitors with her flamboyance. She lived in a small cottage near her mother's house, and for part of her life lived in penury. Lawrence Johnston left her his fortune, and many of his plants, but the gift came too late, and she died soon after.

Vita Sackville-West is the most well-known woman gardener of this century, although as the American writer Eleanor Perényi suggests, this may be as much due to her lifestyle and aristocratic connections, as to her gardening skills. Vita wanted to be a grand landowner, and wrote – improbably in the socialist *New Statesman* – that she had bought several thousand acres of extra land, partly as investment, partly so that when she went for her daily walk she need not leave her own property. She argued that she loved fields and orchards 'so much that I want them to be safely mine'. By today's standards, she made insufferable remarks about the 'servant classes', and her manner was often either imperious or condescendingly gracious.

She wanted to be remembered as a poet, and won the Hawthornden Prize for her poetry, but her work was out of touch with other twentieth-century poets such as W. H. Auden and T. S. Eliot, and in the phrase of another poet,

RIGHT
Vita Sackville-West peering into an urn (right). She is accompanied by her Waterperry-trained head gardeners, Sybil Kreutzberger and Pamela Schwerdt.

RIGHT
Sissinghurst, the creation of Vita Sackville-West and her husband Harold Nicolson, is justifiably famous. This is the gateway into the Rose Garden, showing the border of 'London Pride' irises.

The White Garden as it was in 1943. Perhaps the best known of all the garden rooms which make up Sissinghurst, the plants are all white or grey, and the focal point is a Chinese glazed earthenware vase. Pots, urns and decorative stoneware are a distinctive feature in the garden.

George Barker, she felt she could no longer write 'of a society invented by beach boys and supported by girls without girdles'. She then confined her writing mainly to gardening and turned to her garden for solace, except in July and August when she disliked it, and escaped abroad or to friends.

Her garden at Sissinghurst has been described many times. It is made up of a series of small 'garden rooms' each decorated around a theme, the most famous of which is the White Garden. These small scale pictures or rooms within a larger garden is now a popular style, adopted at Hidcote in Gloucestershire and Tintinhull in Somerset, and in numerous smaller gardens. Vita described her garden as 'a rumpus of colour, a drunkenness of scents'. She became a rose expert, and the garden contains many old French roses, and some extravagant ramblers.

The garden is over-visited, and the wear and tear on grass has been so great that some of the original walks have been replaced with decorated stone paths. There have been other changes to the planting, as plants and shrubs have died or grown too unwieldy. Sissinghurst has had a tradition of female head gardeners from the 1950s. It was then in the competent charge of Sybil Kreutzberger and Pamela Schwerdt, graduates of the Waterperry Gardening

School for Women. The present head gardener, Sarah Cook, continues the tradition.

Tintinhull, a seventeenth-century manor house and garden, was bought by Phyllis Reiss in 1933. It is rated greater than Sissinghurst by modern garden designers and plantsmen such as Lanning Roper, Graham Thomas, and by Sylvia Crowe, the landscape architect (and family friend) who had this to say about it.

> Its particular success lies in the contrast and proportion of its spaces, in the uses of existing trees to pin down and unite the design, and in the beautifully contrived views . . . its planting is probably unique, because it combines the use of very varied species grown naturally, and yet used strictly as elements of design. No plant, however lovely in itself is grown unless it contributes to the picture . . . In spite of restraint it is anything but austere.

Sylvia Crowe was an extremely influential landscape architect; for instance, she advised the Forestry Commission how to use mixed tree planting to make the most of ancient hillsides – advice not always taken. She attempted to define the principles of good design for gardens. For her the essential ingredients are: 'unity, scale, time, space division, light and shade, texture, tone and colour and styles'.

Tintinhull scores highly on the Crowe scale. Light and shade from its great trees are an integral part of the design. The garden is made on flat ground but gives an impression of height and depth. There are two formal pools whose shape and reflections are highlighted by the subtle colouring, textures and patterning of flowers, foliage and paving. Together they make a whole which is more than the sum of the parts; it is difficult to realize, as Lanning Roper said, that Tintinhull covers less than an acre of land.

Phyllis Reiss could not have been more different from some of her flamboyant predecessors. Graham Thomas wrote of her:

> Those who have known Mrs Reiss will never forget her kindly spirit, and all others who visit her garden will have much to thank her for. Through her garden she shares with all of us her skill, her happiness and her love of beauty.

RIGHT
The borders at Montacute in Somerset were designed by Phyllis Reiss. She chose strong colours: purples, yellows and dark reds, to offset the imposing yellow Ham-stone house.

RIGHT
Phyllis Reiss' own garden at Tintinhull was calm, peaceful and restrained, and cleverly designed to give elevation and a sense of distance to a small flat site. This is the small pool garden, planted early in the year with white and cream tulips, which are later succeeded by white roses.

She was both happy and unpretentious. In a rare broadcast for the BBC, she began, 'My garden is, I think and hope, a happy one.' She said she enjoyed growing old, 'now all the flames of life had gone and one was left with the glowing embers of memories and friendship'; and that beauty was 'an antidote to all necessary daily cares'. Tintinhull reflects her serenity and ease with herself.

Besides Tintinhull, Phyllis Reiss was asked to advise on neighbouring Montacute House in Somerset, now also the property of the National Trust. Both Vita Sackville-West and Norah Lindsay visited it and made suggestions but, perhaps because she lived so near, Phyllis Reiss undertook the final design, and replanted Vita's unsuccessful pastel borders. Montacute is a great and imposing Elizabethan house with towering pinnacles, built of the local yellow Ham stone, and surrounded by wide gravel terraces. In Graham Thomas's view, Phyllis Reiss matched the scale and boldness of the house and made a great success of the design.

> She rose to the occasion splendidly and the borders are an outstanding success, alight with strong colours – whether it be purple aubretia and lemon wallflowers, purple clematises flowing through the stone balusters, the red of dahlias and roses in October, or the contrast of the greenery of yucca and bergenia.

Styles of gardens and standards of maintenance change dramatically according to the times, and what is in the height of fashion in one generation is criticized by a second, forgotten by the third – possibly to be rediscovered by the fourth. Are island beds the reincarnation of the Victorian circular beds, and will little garden rooms go out of fashion in favour of open plantings?

In the past, you had to be rich to be noticed. What typifies our own time is the democratization of gardening. The National Gardens Scheme (commonly known as the Yellow Book), the National Trust, the Royal Horticultural Society, photography and, above all, television, have all made gardening a public and visible activity for everyone who has the beginnings of this obsession, or who merely wants their tiny back garden to look respectable. We can all see, visit and be inspired by the most famous gardens, and many of us have the time and relative affluence to develop our own. There are all kinds of garden machinery to lessen the labour of gardening; and all kinds of chemicals, if you want to use them, to help your garden grow and to control the pests. (Even the most organic of gardeners is tempted by slug pellets – slices of turnip just won't do any more.) It is easier now to buy plants. There are hundreds of highly specialized nurseries which stock unusual plants, as well as local plant centres which sometimes sell a surprising range of shrubs, flowers and herbs. The real obsessionals can hold national collections of certain varieties of plants. Women have now gained access to the gardening professions, and one or two have reached the highest positions. It is gardening as a profession we turn to next.

CHAPTER THREE

THE NEW PROFESSIONS

Beautiful gardens do not exist in a vacuum. There is an industry behind them. There are the men and women who find plants and grow or hybridize them; the retailers who sell and distribute the plants; there are the producers of garden tools, machinery, chemicals and garden statuary, pots and furniture; the journalists, writers and photographers who describe and record plants and gardens; the garden designers and the garden theorists who try to define what makes a good garden; those who educate and train gardeners; and those who advance the related sciences of botany, horticulture and landscape architecture. Last, but certainly not least, there are the garden clubs and societies – many hundreds of them, amateur and professional, which provide local or specialist forums for exchanging ideas and seeds or plants.

There are all kinds of gardeners and garden trades. The Royal Horticultural Show at Chelsea, London, is annual witness to the complexity and diversity of the gardening world. How have women made their mark in it?

Gertrude Jekyll is one of the most famous, a garden writer and designer, whose garden at Munstead Wood, Surrey, was a Mecca for gardeners for more than forty years from the 1880s to the 1920s. Her acute observations and theories about colour and design have influenced recent generations of

Helen Allingham, the Edwardian artist who idealized and often sentimentalized cottage gardens, painted this glowing picture of Gertrude Jekyll's herbaceous border at Munstead Wood.

gardeners. She was a friend of Ellen Willmott; together they received the Victoria Medal of Honour from the Royal Horticultural Society in 1897. But whereas Ellen Willmott's influence, like her garden, has vanished, Gertrude Jekyll's dictums on good taste and refinement in the garden still have an almost biblical status.

Gertrude Jekyll regarded herself as a professional; her work was always of the highest standard, she was independent and respected, and she earned a living from her writings and commissions. She was one of the first women students at the School of Art in Kensington in 1862. She was daring. The comfortable and secure Victorian upper-middle-class world to which she belonged was suspicious of such radical steps as advanced training and careers

Gertrude Jekyll in old age. She originally wanted to be a painter, but became instead a talented craftswoman, gilder, wood-carver, embroiderer and photographer, until finally she decided to concentrate on gardening. Her garden at Munstead Wood became a showpiece for her theories on gardening. In later years she became reclusive and discouraged visitors.

for women. But she had her family behind her and she was quietly determined and independent-minded from the beginning. The art training she received was more than meticulous; the first year was spent on perfecting a single drawing. Ladies, however, were not allowed to attend the life classes or see nudes.

Gertrude Jekyll was heavily influenced by the theories of John Ruskin, and the Arts and Crafts Movement led by William Morris; but she carefully avoided involvement in any of the social issues which so concerned them. Utopian socialism was of no interest to her. Similarly, although for many years a close friend of Barbara Bodichon, who was in the vanguard of feminism and an agitator for women's rights, Gertrude remained conservative in her views about the social order. Everything, including people, should be in 'its right and proper place'.

She is often regarded as a champion of homely arts and cottage gardens. She was a friend of Helen Allingham, who stayed at Munstead Wood, and whose warm, glowing and sentimental pictures of cottage gardens, loved by Edwardians, were associated with her. Despite the rosy charm of the Allingham paintings, there was nothing at all cottagey about Gertrude's organized and well-provided lifestyle, or about her 15-acre meticulously tended, extremely well-stocked garden.

She admired craftsmanship, and was herself an accomplished needlewoman, quilter, gilder, silversmith, wood-carver, decorative artist and photographer, as well as a gardener, but despite these wide-ranging talents, she deplored any departure from tradition, sobriety and good order. Her life, like her garden, was carefully crafted.

It was only in her late forties that she gave up most of her arts and crafts and devoted herself almost exclusively to gardening. She was already well-known as a gardener but once she bought Munstead Wood it became her workshop. She began theorizing. Gardening, she argued, was 'painting a picture'. Colours should be placed 'with careful forethought and deliberation as a painter employs them on his picture and not dropped down in lifeless dabs, as he has them on his palette.' They should be in drifts, following the spectrum; contrasts subtle rather than strident. Her tone was always lofty, and drew upon abstract moral values.

RIGHT
Edward Lutyens was the only person who dared to caricature Gertrude Jekyll, and to tease her about her self-importance.

BELOW RIGHT
The garden at Hestercombe, which is one of Gertrude Jekyll's best-known and well-preserved designs.

No artificial planting can equal that of nature but one may learn from it that great lesson of moderation and reserve and simplicity of intent and directness of purpose, and the inestimable value of the quality called 'breadth'.

Dignity, restraint, repose and refinement were the words she used over and over again to describe gardening.

By the 1880s Gertrude Jekyll was writing for William Robinson's magazine *The Garden,* and for a church magazine called *The Guardian,* and judging at horticultural shows. She had been collecting rare plants for some time, and hybridizing. She knew all the gardeners, gardening writers and botanical artists of her time, although, as her biographer Sally Festing comments, she did not like socializing, and did not want to waste her time 'talking to people she did not care about on subjects which did not interest her'.

At the age of 46, and already established in her gardening career, she met the 19-year-old Edwin Lutyens. She was enchanted by him; he was boyishly amusing, cajoling and affectionate. He, in turn, admired her worldliness and her skills. He became a regular weekend visitor. Only with him was she informal or relaxed; for him, she was 'Aunt Bumps' or 'Mabs – Mother of All bulbs'; for everyone else, 'Miss Jekyll'. Together they went looking at and photographing houses, farms and cottages, noting their construction methods and the local stone and brick industries which supported them. She hated tawdriness; buildings should have 'simplicity of purpose' and 'be built to endure', to be 'the best and rightest thing'. She obtained commissions for Lutyens from her friends and acquaintances, and commissioned him to build her own house on her land at Munstead Wood. For both of them a house and garden were integral, and their partnership is legendary.

Gertrude Jekyll produced designs for over 350 gardens; more often for a feature such as an island bed or herb garden, rather than the whole garden. She did not like visiting the sites but would request precise site details, and then send her plan to the owners. Often there was a correspondence about her proposals. Some of the gardens were designed with Lutyens, although many

were her commissions alone. On the other hand, Lutyens almost always sent her his architectural commissions for comment, whether or not she undertook to design the garden.

Her writing also made her famous. She wrote 14 books and over 2000 articles. Much of her work is still in print or has been reproduced as anthologies. Apart from her measured and slightly sanctimonious tone, what is so striking is the quality of her observations. Here she is, writing about juniper in February:

> It has very little of positive green; a suspicion of warm colour in the shadowy hollows, and a blue-grey bloom of the tenderest quality imaginable on the outer masses of foliage. Each tiny blade-like leaf has a band of dead palest bluish-green colour on the upper surface, edged with a narrow line of dark green with slight polish; it looks as if the green back had been brought up over the edge of the leaf to make the dark edging on its upper surface . . . This arrangement of mixed colouring and texture, and infinitely various position of the little spiny leaves, allows the eye to penetrate unconsciously a little way into the mass, so that one sees as much tender shadow as actual leaf surface, and this is probably the cause of the wonderfully delicate and, so to speak, intangible quality of colouring.

To see so subtly and to describe so carefully is indeed a craft, and she worked at it all her life.

Her special success and her reputation were inspiring, although she made no claims to beat a path for other women. She did, however, lend her name to and became patron of one of the first of the women's gardening schools, the Glynde School for Lady Gardeners set up by Lady Frances Wolseley. Lady Frances learnt much of her gardening from William Robinson, whom she first met in 1888 when she was 16.

The gardening school was set up in 1904 with two students. It was never very big, and did not last very long, but its graduates were highly regarded – Gertrude Jekyll tried to secure employment for them on her commissions. Lady Frances came from a military family, and the school was run on military lines. There were many rules and many punishments for breaking them. Even so, one of her former students wrote of her:

RIGHT
Lady Frances
Wolseley who
believed in running
her gardening
school along
military lines.

BELOW
Pupils from the
Glynde School for
Lady Gardeners
being instructed in
a field of sweet
peas.

[She was] a great pioneer as well as a great woman and a great gardener
. . . By founding a horticultural college, by writing many books, by
originating propaganda, she did much for women workers on the land.

The Glynde School was a small part of a wider movement for careers for
women. As early as 1870, the *Gardener's Chronicle* carried articles about the
Gardening School for Women in Boston, U.S.A., and there ensued some
strong articles and editorials:

Would you have women plough and dig and cart muck? . . . No more would
I have women scrub floors and spend their days at the washtub . . . or baking
pies . . . I would let brawn do the drudgery and brain the fine work in all
trades.

Studley College for Women, founded in 1898, was another initiative for
women. Its founder, the Countess of Warwick, was a contemporary of Jekyll
and Wolseley, but much more controversial than either of them. She was a
society beauty, a staunch feminist and socialist and a well-known philanthropist. She also had loose morals – by Victorian standards – and maintained a
notorious friendship with the Prince of Wales. Her reputation obscured her
achievements and her very real concern about women's position in horticulture and agriculture. She founded the *Women's Agricultural Times* in 1899, as the
official journal of the Lady Warwick Agricultural Association for Women. The
journal was linked to a women's employment agency and published particulars
of jobs, including work in the colonies. She raised money from her rich friends,
including the King, Winston Churchill, Mrs Asquith and Cecil Rhodes, to
open Studley College in Warwickshire.

The enterprise flourished, with modern laboratories, residential wings, and
an annual intake of 100 students. Women were trained at varying levels in
agriculture and horticulture. Lady Warwick found the vision easier than the
practical details and there were continual financial problems although the
College did manage to attract substantial grants from the Ministry of Food
and Agriculture. It awarded nationally recognized certificates, and had
academically as well as horticulturally qualified staff. The college was wound
up in 1967, ironically for the same reason as it was founded, because it was

The Countess of Warwick, society belle and imperious feminist campaigner, inaugurating Studley College in 1903. The college was located in a large, but neglected estate in Warwickshire, complete with mock-Victorian castle and home farm.

only for women. Government grants were withdrawn as it was felt that avenues for women in horticulture were now open; no more pioneering was considered necessary.

Swanley Horticultural College in Kent was the earliest of the colleges, and exceptional in that it was co-educational. It opened in 1885, for men, and in 1891 admitted the first women. There were excited articles about it in the *Gardener's Chronicle*: 'The institution is unique in the educational system'. By 1899 the women outnumbered men heavily, and by 1902 the last of the men left and it became a women's college. In 1908 there is a record of Swanley students joining in women's suffrage marches.

> It was agreed by the Governors that they might walk as women gardeners but it was undesirable that they should use the college name.

Swanley's record was distinguished. It managed to attract grants and scholarships from Kent County Council and had some Ministry of Education funding as well. For many years the principal was an ex-student, Dr Kate Barratt, a reputed scientist. The college offered courses to degree level, and was popularly known as the 'brain place'. It disappeared only in 1939, when it was amalgamated with London University's Wye College.

The Kew girls, taken on in 1896,
looking distinguished in their brown knickerbocker suits.
Despite their sober attire,
they caused a sensation.

Sir William Thistleton-Dyer, the Director of the Royal Botanic Gardens, Kew, came under considerable pressure to take Swanley graduates, and in 1896 the first women staff were taken on. So as not to be conspicuous, they had to wear brown knickerbocker suits like boys, but this misfired, and crowds flocked to Kew to see them. The satirical magazine *Fun* in 1900 printed these verses entitled 'London Kewriosity'.

> They gardened in bloomers, the newspapers said;
> So to Kew without warning all Londoners sped:
> From the roofs of the buses they had a fine view
> Of the ladies in bloomers who gardened at Kew.
>
> The orchids were slighted, the lilies were scorned,
> The dahlias were flouted, till botanists mourned,
> But the Londoners shouted, 'What ho, there, Go to;
> Who wants to see blooms now you've bloomers at Kew.'

The Kew girls had a hard time. They also had to remain single. The Kew journal records that one of its first women employees ended her distinguished career by 'taking to herself a husband'.

Dame Sylvia Crowe and Brenda Colvin, pioneers in landscape design, were educated at Swanley. Sylvia Crowe stayed the course, and became a garden designer and then a landscape architect. Brenda Colvin was more critical; she left the course early and hired one of the tutors as her own private teacher. She also became a garden designer. Both were critical of Gertrude Jekyll, whom they regarded as 'whimsical', unprofessional and essentially irrelevant. They were interested in modern materials and innovations – Sylvia Crowe designed a concrete summer house for the Chelsea Flower Show in 1937 and Brenda Colvin helped to set up the Institute of Landscape Architects (founded at the 1928 Chelsea Flower Show). They both argued that gardens were part of a wider pattern of adaptation to the landscape, and should reflect broader concerns rather than individual preferences. Brenda Colvin in her book *Land and Landscape* (1970) argued:

> We should think of this planet Earth as a single organism in which humanity is involved . . . the sense of superior individuality which we enjoy is illusory.

Sylvia Crowe and Brenda Colvin's garden design work led to new commissions; industrial landscapes for factories and power stations; regeneration of decayed industrial sites; design of parks and common land; and forestry planting. Brenda Colvin felt strongly that women needed no special protection:

> I resist segregation of *any* sort and see no necessity for special women's organizations, as it seems to me that we exert a far greater influence on mixed bodies than is possible from opposing organizations.

Frances Perry, now in her eighties, the first woman vice-president of the R.H.S., and a holder of the Victoria Medal of Honour, was also a graduate of Swanley. She lived next door to E. A. Bowles, the famous plantsman, who was a misogynist. 'I look upon you as one of my boys,' he told the eager young Frances. An enthusiast since visiting the Chelsea Flower Show at the age of 13, she wanted a horticultural career. Bowles insisted she should train – 'you can't do it without proper training' – and approved the Swanley prospectus for her. Although scholarships were available, the fees for Swanley were £300 a year and there was a varied collection of students; some genuinely interested, some recuperating divorcees, some filling in time before being presented at court. There was rigorous boarding-school discipline but much fun and camaraderie.

After leaving Swanley in 1925, Frances obtained a job at the famous nursery firm of Perry, against some opposition from the male staff. She married the son of the owner, specialized in water plants, and wrote a book *Water Gardening* that is still a standard reference. She exhibited for the firm at the Royal Horticultural Shows.

> They were magnificent stands in the early days . . . [The shows] were a social occasion – the men were in grey morning suits and toppers, the women wore hats like Ascot.

There was considerable sniggering at her presence from the male nurserymen at the shows. She remembers how another woman who wore bloomers was the butt of some cruel jokes: 'We came in at the beginning and we had it rough.' Despite this, she persevered and continued working even after her marriage

Frances Perry, a graduate of Swanley College and a distinguished nurserywoman, lecturer and gardening journalist.

and the birth of her sons. She became a lecturer at a horticultural college, and then a broadcaster. Her friendly manner and soft country burr were an instant success on television, and for many years she hosted gardening programmes, as well as becoming principal of the college, and writing books and articles. This was the early days of television, and conditions were primitive. As Frances Perry recalled:

> McDonald Hobley wore a dinner jacket and old sneakers and pants, because they only focussed on the top half. The heat in the studio was terrible. They always said I was too brown so they put yellow stuff all over my face. The plants had a nasty habit of wilting, we had to keep them under a bench and brought them out at the last minute. The programme went out live and there was no rehearsal.

RIGHT
Beatrix Havergal, the formidable founder of Waterperry School for Lady Gardeners. She invariably wore a uniform of green socks, green smock, white shirt with a starched collar and brown tie.

BELOW RIGHT
Waterperry students digging in manure in unison in the south field. Their working day began at 7 a.m. or earlier.

When she was 60, Frances Perry was invited to join the R.H.S. council. According to Roy Hay (whom she later married), this was because there were complaints at the A.G.M., repeated in *The Times*, that there were no women on the R.H.S. Council. The President, Lord Aberconway, blustered and said 'No woman is good enough. What shall I do?' Roy Hay persuaded him to invite Frances Perry, 'She is a splendid, nice person to get on with, everyone who has worked with her loves her and I think you would be wise to send for her.' When she was invited, Frances wrote a dignified letter back.

> If you want me because I am a woman the answer is no, but if you want me because of anything I've done in horticulture, the answer is yes.

Her career continued after retirement. She became an international traveller and world expert on plants, and continued to publish. She helped found Capel Manor Garden, Middlesex, now the gardening centre for the consumer magazine *Which?*. Despite age and infirmity, she is still to be seen at shows, is a frequent traveller abroad, and continues to give talks to groups of gardeners in her unassuming and down-to-earth manner.

Waterperry was undoubtedly the most idiosyncratic of the gardening schools for women. It was set up by Beatrix Havergal and Avice Sanders in

1927. Miss Havergal trained at Thatcham, a small and short-lived gardening school, and went to work as a head gardener at Downe House, a boarding school for girls. There she met Miss Sanders, and they decided to set up for themselves. Miss Havergal was big, had very large feet shod in well-polished lace-ups, close-cut hair, and invariably wore the Thatcham uniform of thick green socks over green breeches, a green smock, a green baize blazer with brass buttons for cold weather, a white shirt with a starched collar and a brown tie. She insisted on daily prayers at which she officiated in a resonant voice. She shared a bedroom with Miss Sanders, who was more self-effacing but equally strict with the girls.

Such was Miss Havergal's personality that her appearance and way of life seemed beyond comment to most of her students although, according to Roy Hay, Lord Aberconway regarded her with ambivalence: whilst he admired her gardening reputation and was gentlemanly to her at shows, he was very reluctant to allow her near the inner cabals of the R.H.S. Miss Havergal's

clothes were incidentally the model for Roald Dahl's character 'Miss Trunchball'; he was a visitor at Waterperry.

The school was small, usually 20 or so students in a large draughty house. It was run on familiar boarding-school lines, as a finishing school for upper-class girls who wanted an outdoor life. 'Ideal perhaps for the non-ambitious, and those who wanted a cloistered and happy existence.' As time went on, it broadened its catchment, and a variety of girls enrolled. Like the Glynde school, rules were strict. As Ursula Maddy describes in her study of the school, *Waterperry: A Dream Fulfilled*, if any plant or seedling wilted or died, meetings were held to discuss it:

> . . . all such acts of indifference or negligence must be punished and the only thorough way of so doing is to make each member of the community feel individually affected by the mischief that has been done.

On a practical level the training could not have been more thorough, although theory sometimes had to take second place if the plants or crops needed attention.

> The training will consist of a Theoretical and thoroughly Practical Training in the various branches of Horticulture, including soils and manures, glasshouse management, pruning and garden construction.

The practical training may have been sound, but the administration was hopelessly muddled. Certificates and diplomas were not issued properly, marks often being awarded the evening before graduation; and the library and studying arrangements for students were disorganized. Staff were not properly appointed, and sometimes not properly paid. The cooking, presided over by Miss Sanders, was healthy but institutional. The premises were scrupulously clean. Health and safety were regarded as personal rather than institutional matters, 'all workers were expected to use their common sense; accidents in short were not expected'.

Waterperry today,
showing mature planting
in the herbaceous borders.

It was a school joke that men were 'a necessary evil', and marriage a betrayal. One of the students, announcing to Miss Havergal her engagement, received the reply, part jest, part outrage, 'But what about the garden?' The only contact with men was the annual visit from the students at Cuddesdon theological college. The students joined in amateur theatricals, but these were eventually discontinued by Cuddesdon as too risqué.

Despite all this, the training was regarded as an extremely thorough grounding in intensive horticulture. For fifteen consecutive years Waterperry won a gold medal at the Chelsea Flower Show for its Royal Sovereign strawberries. This was an enormous effort, and students were diverted from other work. Ursula Maddy writes:

> Weeks before the Day the students had collected tiny hazel twigs, cut them to size and painted them green to make crutches for the fruit, and in this way the stems were supported to above soil level.

Each berry was individually wrapped first in tissue, then in cottonwool, for transporting to Chelsea. Once there, a night-time guard had to be arranged for the exhibits, 'the chief marauders being on-duty policemen and the blackbirds'.

Despite the idiosyncrasies of the school, it produced some remarkable students. The school was essentially Miss Havergal's fiefdom and when she retired it finished. The last intake was in 1969. Waterperry is now a garden centre, and the study block a tea-room, although some of the staff from Miss Havergal's day are still employed in the glasshouses and garden. The famous Royal Sovereign strawberries have now been superseded by other more manageable varieties and are hard to come by.

One of the most distinguished of Waterperry students, Valerie Finnis, stayed on to become a member of staff. Her mother was a keen gardener, and developed the Constance Finnis strain of Iceland poppies. Valerie Finnis was fascinated with plants from an early age. She was at school at Downe House, where Miss Havergal had once worked, and it seemed a natural progression to go to Waterperry. This was in wartime, when vegetable production was important; she and another girl maintained a 25-acre field of vegetables and fruit. She learnt how to make hot-beds and potato clamps, to dig thoroughly, hoe effectively and to drive a tractor. She loved the feel of the loamy soil and its productiveness. It was absorbing but grinding work; in season rising at 3a.m. to drive a four-ton truck with fruit to Covent Garden Market in London.

After the war Valerie Finnis started to grow alpines, specializing in saxifrages. 'I was so thrilled when I rooted my first cutting; I built up the alpine nursery and it just went on.' She became a familiar figure in gardening circles, extraordinarily enthusiastic, idiosyncratic, dramatic and knowledgeable. 'Every single week-end I went to a garden and exchanged plants. When you think of nothing else but plants you get known.'

She stayed with Margery Fish, received buckets of plants from Nancy Lindsay (disintegrating zinc buckets, with Turkish fag-ends amongst the plants), became a close friend of Bill McKenzie (then curator of the Chelsea Physic Garden), and exchanged plants with all the leading gardeners of her generation – Percy Picton (one of William Robinson's gardeners); G. P. Baker; Jimmy Platt; Clarence Elliott, the alpinist; Amy Doncaster, a distinguished neighbour of Roy Lancaster in Hampshire; Joyce, Lady Amory at Knightshayes – all the names from a gardener's *Who's Who*. These exchange networks were a way of conserving plants. It was a rule of thumb always to give away bits of the rarest plants to others in the network, because then they would have a better chance of surviving.

One of Valerie Finnis' patrons was Cecilia Christie-Miller, who had also once been a pupil at Downe House, and who had first interested her in saxifrages. Miss Miller quietly donated money to Waterperry, and persuaded Miss Havergal to purchase an alpine house for the rapidly growing collection of alpines. Later she left Valerie Finnis her collection of plants in her will (which were passed on to Waterperry). E. B. Anderson, one-time President of the Alpine Society, also bequeathed her a *Rhodothamnus chamaecistus*, a rare peat-loving alpine which still thrives in her garden.

Valerie Finnis became a leading plant photographer, and sold her flower portraits all over the world. She was self-taught: 'It was too easy for words.' At the time few other people were using photographs, and she sold her photos to Gordon Fraser cards and Fisons, as well as to journals and magazines. Her gardening work and her photography led to many commissions, and to lecturing (she never spoke for more than 40 minutes on principle, because she

RIGHT
Valerie Finnis and pug Sophie by the 'Constance Finnis' strain of poppies.

BELOW
Valerie Finnis and her husband David Scott, the distinguished plantsman, in their Northamptonshire garden in 1978.

RIGHT
The cosy potting-shed where Valerie Finnis and David Scott potted up thousands of seedlings for their open days. Her hat, one of many, has lyrebird feathers.

feared boring her audience), and for two years she undertook the famous Swan Hellenic cruises. She had emergency lessons from Chris Brickell at the R.H.S.'s gardens at Wisley, Surrey, in order to identify Greek flowers and face 'the terrifying botany mistresses' who came on the tours in large numbers. She provided slides to illustrate her commentaries but was banned by the tour operators from using her slide of a mandrake root, since the root resembled male genitalia. Usually the tours were guided by 'a man from Kew and his wife', so, as a woman on her own, it was sometimes arduous, being botanist and social hostess together.

Valerie Finnis was based at Waterperry, working a 12-hour day, and at the very centre of gardening networks for 28 years. Then at the age of 46 she married Sir David Scott, a distinguished plantsman, and romantically created a garden with him in Northamptonshire.

Their garden and their partnership has become gardening legend. Sir David Scott continued to develop his collection of rare shrubs and trees, and Valerie Finnis relocated her extensive collection of alpines in their walled garden. She also continued to grow vegetables and fruit, which she could not do without. The garden was meticulously hand-weeded, and any promising seedling was nursed and encouraged; in this way 32 new varieties of shrubs and plants were put forward for identification and award. They propagated more than 10,000 plants a year for their open days under the National Gardens Scheme. Each open day attracted more than 1500 visitors (except one year, when it snowed and only 400 appeared), who arrived from all over England to see the garden and buy plants that were available nowhere else. Valerie Finnis was awarded the Victoria Medal of Honour, one of that very select band of women gardeners, which includes Gertrude Jekyll and Ellen Willmott.

Since the death of her husband, Valerie Finnis has decided to disperse some of her own collection to botanic gardens, nurseries and to avid plant collectors. Alpines require more care and maintenance than many other types of plants and she felt that in her late sixties, and on her own, she could no longer look after them to the standard to which they were accustomed. The door of her bedroom is covered with index cards, each with a photo and a record of the progress of every student gardener who has benefited from the Merlin trust, set up in her husband's memory to help young gardeners gain new experiences. Her scrapbook-albums contain photographs of and comments from her many visitors; children are encouraged to draw in them. She likes oddness and oddities. Her cavernous rooms and corridors are covered with paintings by friends, and photographs of plants and gardeners cut out from magazines; there are jars of flowers on tables and ledges; and she cooks her own vegetables and fruit for lunch. Her conversation is a stream of racy and quixotic reminiscences and gardeners' gossip. She is modest about her talents and her own contribution, and worries that she is too tangential, too forgetful and too quirky, 'a grasshopper mind' as she puts it. In fact she is a shrewd observer of the gardening scene, as her fellow judges at the R.H.S. shows know well.

To paraphrase her philosophy of gardening: good gardeners are sloggers, and gardening is about getting your hands dirty. A professional gardener must be directly involved with his or her plants, know them inside out, and understand every variation in their appearance and performance:

> I couldn't stand it, not doing [the gardening] myself . . . I couldn't possibly not have propagated the plants – the satisfaction . . . I couldn't ever be away for more than two days from the plants . . . I don't know how people could leave them behind.

Gardening has been her life; all her friends have come through gardening. 'I've been terribly spoilt with friends.'

Susan Dickinson was one of the last intake of Waterperry students, and is someone whom Valerie Finnis has helped on her way. Now the head gardener at Lord Rothschild's Eythrop estate near Aylesbury, Buckinghamshire, she feels the training in intensive horticulture served her well, although she describes Miss Havergal as 'old-fashioned'. The training was 'a tremendous shock' physically, having to start work at 7a.m. and undertake tasks such as cleaning pots and frames on cold, dark, winter mornings. After Waterperry, she worked in an Irish garden, where the owner was so obsessive that he dug up all his bulbs every three years in order to count them. Then she went as a student to Belgium, to the Arboretum Kalmthout near Antwerp. The cosmopolitan staff and the genial atmosphere helped her to rethink some of her attitudes: 'It was a philosophy of life, of enjoyment, rather than just work.'

Susan Dickinson,
head gardener at Eythrop and graduate of Waterperry,
with one of her extravagantly planted ornamental pots.

Sue Minter, Curator of the Chelsea Physic Garden, and one of the first women to hold a senior managerial post in professional gardening circles. Before coming to Chelsea she was in charge of the Palm House at Kew.

She also learnt about the relationship between garden produce and good food, how to handle vegetables and salads creatively in the kitchen.

She held a variety of jobs and then worked for Esther Merton at the Old Rectory in Burghfield, Berkshire, which she enjoyed immensely. This was a personal plant collection, and she found herself very much in sympathy with the style of her employer. The huge terrace pots of flowers they created were widely featured in gardening magazines. From Burghfield she went to Eythrop. Here with a staff of six she manages a large walled garden, newly laid out for fruit and vegetable production, as well as for flowers. Around the house are Victorian bedding schemes, lawns, woodland areas and a lake.

> I didn't like not to do everything myself. You have to plan for an 8-hour day outside, and you are so dependent on the weather. The garden is divided up, everyone has their own area, and if someone is pushed, someone else will help out.

Whatever the vision and involvement of the owner, the working life of a gardener is prosaic and professional. It depends on the generosity of the employer how much scope and credit is given to the gardener; sometimes a great deal, sometimes very little.

93

One of the most senior women gardeners in Britain is Sue Minter, Curator of the Chelsea Physic Garden in London. Like many of the women featured in this book, she was a keen gardener from childhood. She had her first glasshouse at 11, and was specializing in chrysanthemums by the age of 14. But her family and school thought gardening was not a proper career so she read history at Cambridge. She took a job in publishing but knew she wanted to go back to gardening. She took her basic National Certificate in Horticulture under a government-sponsored scheme and started work in commercial horticulture, as a buyer for a nursery. Then she took advantage of another retraining scheme, and obtained the M.Hort., the most advanced qualification in horticulture, coming top in her year.

After working in a gardening centre, she went to Kew in 1982 as a propagator in the temperate nursery. She was promoted to supervisor of the palm house, and oversaw its restoration. This was a major project, replanning the planting, nursing the plants during the alterations, offering a new educational emphasis in the display, and an interpretation of the economics of plants. She worked to a restoration committee, and had to explain and justify her decisions to them, and execute theirs. She wrote a book about the palm house, which has been a gardening best-seller.

At Chelsea Physic Garden, one of the oldest gardens in Britain, she is not only responsible for the plant collections and displays, but also for the financial viability of the garden. Like Kew, the Physic Garden now has to be financially self-sufficient. This means developing the lettings side, allowing more openings to the public, and increasing publicity for the garden. The garden, for the first time, will be selling plants propagated from the rare collections housed there.

Today it is comparatively easy to gain a gardening qualification. The Institute of Horticulture provides leaflets on courses and job opportunities. Students can work in environmental horticulture, landscape design and construction, and in private estates and specialist gardens, in commercial production and in the horticultural press. Five universities offer degrees in horticulture and related sciences; twenty-eight colleges specialize in horticultural training. There are City and Guild courses, correspondence courses, amenity courses, evening courses. Kew and Wisley both offer horticultural training. Kew first admitted women students in 1954; Wisley, the last bastion, in 1973.

Jenny Webber is a gardener working in the parks department of a London borough. She was a manual worker, then became interested in gardening and managed to transfer to the parks department, which seconded her to a City and Guilds horticultural course. She is in charge of a small park, 'not a classy park', where she undertakes general maintenance, cutting, pruning and some planting. She has a small hut in the park where she keeps her tools and can make a cup of tea. She argued for a 'no chemicals' policy, and managed to have all spraying banned. She thinks public gardens are an important resource for the people who live nearby.

> I like being a public servant, the relationships with people in the park, I don't want to be a private gardener . . . if I don't know a kid it wouldn't take me long to find out who they are and where they live . . . I know the winos, the dog walkers, the people who cut through, the locals who like to sit . . . And people are very appreciative. I can give advice to people who back on to the park, I cut the grass and hedges for old ladies, give cuttings . . . I'm not supposed to, but why not do a bit extra, it doesn't hurt.

Unfortunately, her job is about to be abolished. Contract workers, travelling by lorry from park to park, and using chemical sprays to keep down weeds, are more economical. As in many local authority parks and gardens, the personal touch for plants or people is too expensive, and the grass will be cut and the shrubs pruned according to an unalterable schedule drawn up by people who have no personal knowledge of what is involved. The municipal gardens, such a source of pride in Victorian times, and occasionally enterprising in their employment of women, are no longer a source of inspiration or interest.

Gardening is more than a hobby, it is also a livelihood and an occupation. It is still slightly easier to seek and find promotion and renown as a man; but women are widely respected too. We have come a long way since Gertrude Jekyll trained as an artist.

CHAPTER FOUR

FAMILY FORTUNES

Are gardeners born and not made? Where does it come from, the impetus to garden? Many of the women described in this book give credit to their mothers – Alicia Amherst, Ellen Willmott and her sister Rose, Nancy Lindsay, Valerie Finnis. They were taught to grow flowers before they could read. Others remember a fascination with plants and their arrangement from their earliest years, a sensitivity to the flowers, shrubs and trees around them, both wild and cultivated, an uncontrollable instinct to garden. Gertrude Jekyll remembered from childhood the intensity and gravity of her feelings about flowers.

> I rejoice when I see anyone, and especially children, inquiring about flowers and wanting gardens of their own . . . for the love of gardening is a seed that once sown never dies, but always grows and grows to an enduring and ever-increasing source of happiness.

Others trace their obsession with gardening to a general education in the arts, having a familiarity with painting, sculpture and architecture, and seeing the garden as the greatest challenge to their artistic imagination.

Like all nature-nurture debates there is no single answer to how an obsession takes hold; there are probably as many reasons as there are gardeners. But it

A tantalizing glimpse of the sunken garden
at Kiftsgate Court.

is possible to discern trends, to suggest there is a pattern of inspiration prompted by circumstance. Kiftsgate Court is one such example, a continuity, partly accidental, partly deliberate, which has lasted over three generations of gardening women.

Kiftsgate Court is a Victorian mansion with a transplanted Georgian façade, built on a superb hillside site near Chipping Campden in Gloucestershire. Its current owners politely deprecate their contribution, and maintain that their story is as much luck as judgement.

The garden was started in the 1920s by Heather Muir. She wrote very little, even letters, and she disliked being photographed, and her sense of privacy meant that memoirs of her, outside her immediate family, are rare. Her daughters describe her, in that high-society Edwardian context, as being 'not terribly social . . . going to Royal Ascot, being seen, that didn't interest her one jot'. Her first love was riding and hunting, until an accident in 1922 made her give it up. It was then she concentrated on the garden.

She was the nearest neighbour and a close friend of Lawrence Johnston, the creator of Hidcote Manor Garden, who was also taciturn about his gardening. They were part of a wealthy Cotswold set, whose activities have been documented by the gardening historian Jane Brown. They were concerned with the decoration of country houses and gardens, interiors as well as exteriors,

A rare picture of Heather Muir tending her garden at Kiftsgate Court. By then the garden was already 30 years old.

and enjoyed a style of life which was lively but not unconventional, and which focused on the satisfaction to be had from property and countryside.

Kiftsgate Court was bought by the Muirs in 1918. It had a small paved formal garden in front of the portico of the mansion, surrounded by grassy fields, and a steeply sloped wooded bank falling away from it to the south. The site was promising, the garden virtually non-existent. Johnston was a frequent visitor. He and Heather Muir discussed and experimented with colour and designs, inside and out. They were interested in avant-garde and art nouveau decoration, and Johnston painted a mural for her on the dining room wall (the mural has since been removed to Hidcote). He was laconic, never without a toothpick; she was elegant and formal, and in the words of her daughter 'tried to do whatever she did beautifully'. He threw extravagant and artistic parties, and tolerated his neighbour's small daughters running around (unlike another visitor, Nancy Lindsay, who they describe as having no use for children at all). Mr Muir, who was twenty years older than his wife, was very quiet, easy-going and witty, and not interested in gardening. He would sometimes be 'sent off' to weed the nettles in the wood but played very little part in the restoration of Kiftsgate; Heather Muir was the dominant character.

Gradually, Heather Muir transformed the garden. Kiftsgate first attracted public notice with an article in the 1951 R.H.S. journal, from the most eminent garden critic of all, Graham Stuart Thomas. By the time he saw the garden in the 1950s, it bore no relation to its original state. In his article Graham Stuart Thomas wrote in superlatives.

> Set in this combination of natural beauty and interesting planting the garden can but remind one of a brilliant jewel; for such it is, with a facet to suit the taste of every visitor.

The north-facing side of the house was covered with climbing shrubs: ivies, *Akebia quinata*, *Hydrangea petiolaris*, viburnum and magnolia. The south-facing side of the house was dominated by a 27-foot *Rosa banksiae* 'Lutea', the floriferous little double yellow rose, with lovely foliage, which really was a spectacular sight in flower, a wall of sunlight. The garden had been extended and terraced. The original small garden had become a parterre, divided into four sections, each edged with box and planted informally with paeonies,

RIGHT
Delphiniums and
Rosa 'Graham
Thomas' in the
yellow border.
Graham Thomas
wrote about the
border, and the rose
is planted in his
honour.

BELOW
The imposing
Georgian façade to
Kiftsgate Court.
Many tender plants
are trained against
the walls, or shelter
at the foot of them.

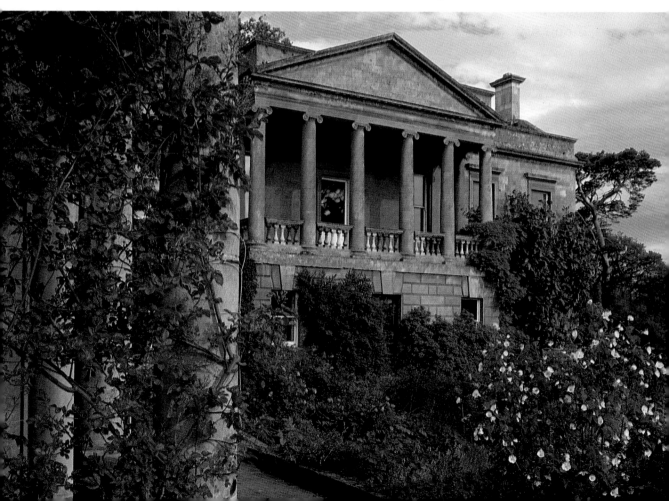

lavenders and less common plants. A sundial stood in the middle of the parterre. Below the parterre was a long grass walk, with glorious flower borders eight feet wide. Graham Stuart Thomas commented rapturously that it was:

> . . . the finest piece of skilled colour work coupled with good cultivation and horticultural interest that it has yet been my pleasure to see . . . a great diversity of plant forms and yet the resulting blend is one of soft beauty.

At the end of the wide flower border, there were steps leading to a second long border. This border was planted in much darker colours, with more emphasis on foliage. Whereas the first border was, in Graham Stuart Thomas' words, 'a lady's boudoir of greys, pinks and mauves', the second border was 'more masculine . . . it also has an eastern splendour and a richness of plant form of a most unusual quality'. There was also a third border, 70 feet long, consisting solely of the old striped rose, *Rosa mundi*. 'The brilliant and bizarre effect of this pink and crimson striping from literally thousands of blooms was a rare sight.'

The wooded slope had been partially terraced and planted with rare shrubs, offering spectacular views through the leaves. Finally, back at the top, on the third side of the house, below a veranda, was a sunken white garden, bordered at the back by a hedge of skimmia. As one of her daughters comments, 'she was a creative genius'.

Heather Muir's two daughters were brought up at home by a governess, whose skill at drawing and whose knowledge of wild flowers they remember fondly. 'If she had been allowed to go ahead she would have been a top politician or had a career. But in those days all you could do was to be a governess.' The girls were keen horse-riders and not much interested in gardening. They were aware of their mother's interest, and sometimes, but without pressure, she would try to get them to do small jobs. 'Oh pull out that weed for me . . . just hold this branch a minute . . .' They have some vivid memories. Heather Muir preferred plants that caused no trouble, that did not need staking, pruning or spraying. On one occasion she said tartly to Graham Stuart Thomas, 'You might become a good gardener if you learn to leave your secateurs at home,' which became a family joke. They also remember ordering the plants; the packages that came from Veitch and Bunyard, the most famous nurserymen of the day.

Both daughters left home and moved to London. Diany Binny moved back to Kiftsgate with her own two daughters in 1954 and overlapped with her mother for a while. There were major alterations to the building, and a wing was removed to make a gravelled forecourt. Her sister, Miss Muir, who remained single, moved to a house nearby in the village. For five years after her mother's death Diany was afraid to touch anything in the garden.

> I never changed anything for five years and the garden went backwards, of course . . . I mean you've got to keep on doing things and I didn't dare. I kept on feeling my mother looking over my shoulder saying, 'Oh, I don't think I'd like that'.

She learnt from experience and gained confidence. She refused to read gardening books.

> There's nothing more awful than gardening books . . . I never read them because I don't agree with them . . . I think it's no good listening to everybody . . . you become a little bit of everything and it doesn't work. It's rather like a painter, I think, you've got to have your own ideas.

The first innovation was the semi-circular swimming pool at the bottom of the slope, doubling up as an ornamental pool. Then two statues were commissioned, one placed under a clipped sorbus arch at the end of the rose walk. In the white garden there is now a small pool with a fountain, and some new colours have been introduced, and new shrubs planted. Some of the older shrubs were performing unexpectedly; in particular a rose bought as *Rosa moschata* had reached a spread of 80 by 90 feet and had almost suffocated the copper beech through which it was climbing. The rose was recognized as an original seedling and renamed by Graham Stuart Thomas – now a friend and regular visitor – as *Rosa filipes* 'Kiftsgate'. (This rose, whose vigour has science-fiction qualities, has become one of the best-known of climbing roses, and is widely available.) Despite the changes and alterations, the existing structure and design remained; the guardianship of the garden, although problematic, was much easier than starting from scratch.

Heather Muir had had a team of gardeners to instruct. By the 1970s labour was scarcer and more expensive and Diany Binny, although she had two full-time gardeners, was herself, of necessity, a labouring gardener. Her sister also helped with the weeding. Visitors would meet Diany Binny dressed in trousers and headscarf, and stout shoes, giving her forthright opinions on the plants she sold. The garden had been opened occasionally for the National Gardens Scheme but they decided to open it commercially.

> I can't remember what we charged, I think one and sixpence . . . And we had the most ghastly sort of plants we used to sell . . . and then it grew because people wanted to come, so I suppose we thought well, might as well open a bit more . . . and then we sort of decided to sell more plants and get better plants . . . now it's an essential part of keeping the garden.

This reminiscence is a double one, for Diany Binny's daughter Anne Chambers was now involved. Like her mother before her, she had not consciously been interested in gardening.

> I enjoyed the garden and we used to go round and mum used to point out names of various things which probably stuck subconsciously, but I didn't want to be a gardener . . . I had lots of other lives to lead and things to do in London . . . it's a sort of middle-aged past-time . . . and I haven't done any training either except for mum bossing me and telling me what to do . . . Luckily the garden wasn't pushed on me, so as a result I grew into it and wanted to come back and live here.

Anne Chambers came back with her husband and three young children, and became a gardener alongside her mother. Her husband Johnny was at first a spectator but was gradually drawn in, first of all providing computerized stock-lists, and then propagating. He admires the closeness between Anne and Diany, and the way in which jobs are shared out between them.

> Diany is the grand designer, the one who keeps us on the straight and narrow . . . but otherwise it's by subtle negotiation . . . these two are very careful about what they allow each other to do! When Anne tries to plant something that Diany wants there is the most awful row!

LEFT
Anne Chambers
and Diany Binny
discussing tactics in
the garden.

RIGHT
The beautiful *Rosa
gallica*-walk
culminating in a
sorbus arch framing
a modern statue.

BELOW
Another glimpse of
the yellow border,
which consists
mainly of foliage,
highlighted with
pure blue
delphiniums, and
yellow and orange
flowers, like this
orange hemerocallis.

This remark amuses both Anne and her mother. One completes the sentences that the other has begun, and they laugh a great deal. The garden is changing again. The steep bank needs replanting, and the original wooden sleepers which terrace the slope have to be replaced gradually, a 'devilish' job. Diany can no longer undertake heavy labour, and is busy in the top part, whilst Anne and her husband undertake the work on the slope.

For many years Diany has taken her holidays with her sister, who lives nearby, and whose own garden is cleverly laid out and very colour conscious, in the family tradition. 'I could never keep my hands out of the earth . . . I started seriously in 1971 with just a field.' She orders plants and visits gardens with her sister, and they swop specimens. For a time, until her tragic murder, their companion on many of their trips was Hilda Murrell, the well-known nurserywoman, who by then had retired and had come to hate the roses that had made her famous. Miss Muir, whose small garden is also open to the public, feels that the gardening public is well-educated, and deserves respect.

> The average gardening public is more intelligent, shops around, knows names . . . it's wrong to be critical, most gardens have something of interest somewhere.

Burghfield Rectory in Berkshire is another garden which attracts flocks of visitors. The garden belongs to Esther Merton and her husband. Esther Merton, like many of the women in this book, came to gardening late in life.

> Once you get over into your forties and you've had hundreds of children and been married a few times and all the rest of it, you suddenly think there must be more to life than this! You then get your fingers into the earth . . . now my daughter's doing the same thing. She used to say 'Oh God Mum, all we ever see of you is your bottom sticking out of a border, it's boring.'

Despite ill-health, and interruptions, Esther Merton has been obsessionally developing the garden ever since that first revelation. She read copiously to educate herself. Margery Fish was her inspiration.

> I loved Mrs Fish, I adored her. Mrs Fish wrote about her garden, it was fabulous and I loved it because she made mistakes the whole time and she

used to write the wrong thing in her books and it was lovely to find she had made mistakes, it wasn't just you that was hopeless.

She made two herbaceous borders 60 yards long between yew hedges. Behind one of the hedges is a small swimming pool. The borders lead down to a wilder part of the garden and to the large pool, which is planted round with azaleas and the giant pink meadowsweet. Around the shady side of the house, there are white and green plants, hellebores, green nicotiana, daphnes and hydrangeas. On the terrace are huge urns and pots, overflowing with startling combinations of flowers. These pots, like large vases of flowers, were a speciality of Susan Dickinson, who was once the gardener here, and whose influence can still be felt.

Esther Merton was a traveller, and many of her plants were collected from trips abroad. There is a golden raintree, *Koelrueteria paniculata*, a legacy of a garden tour of China; a *Magnolia grandiflora* hybrid from the legendary Princess Sturzda in Normandy; a *Buddleia farreri* grown from a cutting from a plant on Mount Omei.

One of the delights of visiting Burghfield Rectory is Esther Merton's enthusiasm for the garden, and her generosity in sharing her knowledge and experience.

I'm very conscious of the feel of houses and places and the minute I saw this house I knew it was a happy, wonderful place, old contented clergymen and their wives. They probably fought like cats and dogs, but I like to imagine they were all very happy together and it had a lovely happy feel about it, and to me it always has had since.

Her gardening lore is now being passed on to her grandchildren, with whom she spends much time. She has encouraged her five-year-old granddaughter Daisy to cultivate a small garden.

Well, you've got your little apple tree. Minarettes they are, sweet! But I tell you what, I've found some other apple trees we could put round your garden. They're little low ones and they're called stepovers and you plant them round the edge of the beds, don't you think that might be rather fun?

Esther Merton on the terrace at Burghfield Rectory.

Rosy Boase and her mother Irene Feesey are another pair of inseparable gardening companions. Rosy is a primary teacher in Northamptonshire, with four children, the youngest of whom, Mary, is five. They live in a converted Georgian mansion and for the last 17 years Rosy has gardened in part of the grounds, taking care of a romantic avenue an eighth of a mile long, and a section of a walled vegetable garden. Her mother lives in Chelmsford, Essex, and has been developing her small suburban garden since the 1940s. Both gardens overflow with rare and beautiful plants, shared between them for many years.

Irene Feesey, now a sprightly 80, still recollects as a five-year-old being spellbound by wood anemones, and love-in-a-mist. 'I have loved flowers all my life.' She went to art school, nursed during the war, and then married. She stayed at home with her family, and developed her gardening interest by reading.

I loved the old gardening books, I was inspired by the early writers like E. A. Bowles, Gertrude Jekyll and Frances Hope . . . I couldn't afford to buy them so I copied out chunks – I filled 24 notebooks.

Undeterred by cold weather, Irene Feesey and her daughter Rosy Boase discuss where to plant another rare specimen.

Gradually she acquired plants, sending away for precious rare specimens from catalogues, and trying them out in the garden. 'I even wrote a book about neglected plants. I had a very enthusiastic style but no one was interested then.'

Her husband laid out the garden formally, and the children had to 'mind the edges'. She could not drive (and still gets around on a bicycle) and her husband wanted to stay put once he came home from work, so they rarely visited other gardens. They did, however, go on annual trips to Wales. They visited Bodnant Garden and other nearby Welsh gardens, and Irene remembers the magnolias, the camellias and, above all, the eucryphias, the evergreen summer-flowering tree from the southern hemisphere. 'I was so inspired by the eucryphias – they're still my favourite tree.'

She remembers her failures as well as her successes. She obtained a specimen of the rare and beautiful *Paeonia suffruticosa*, 'Rock's Variety', with its large white blooms, maroon centre, and exquisite haunting scent. It is a difficult plant to cultivate, and hers died. Losing it was 'the biggest grief of all . . . I did everything I could but it died. I felt so ashamed.'

The garden now is a little overgrown. There are no more 'edges'; well-established plants have squeezed out some of their neighbours.

> I try to keep the garden nice all year round. There is too much dry shade and shelter. It is too airless, it is difficult to do.

This is not the impression visitors get. Vigorous and unusual, the plants spill over paths and intertwine. Even in late autumn there is form and richness of colour. Inside the house, there are jars of flowers, piles of books, eye-catching home-made objects – like a green papier-mâché bowl decorated with flowers, and collections displayed on shelves. It is the home of a person with flair, or, as Irene describes herself, with humility, 'I think I have a visual eye'.

She gave her daughter Rosy her own tiny plot in the garden when she was seven. But even before that flowers were part of her life. Her birthday cake was always decorated with the little pink-gold 'Perle d'Or' rose. Her brother and sister showed no interest, but Rosy loved her plot.

> I had doll's-house flowers, London pride, miniature things. I enjoyed making more of things. I never played with dolls but I liked to see the plants increasing, the maternal instinct.

Irene took care not to instruct. Rosy adds:

> If she had, I might have shied away. If she had shoved it down my throat I would have dropped it.

Rosy remembers the postman bringing packages from the nurseries. 'I was so jealous of those parcels. I thought, my God, they're only plants.' She remembers, too, the trips to Wales, the smell of the azaleas at Whitsun.

Her interest continued through university and then, when she had her first small garden in Cambridge, her mother helped her clear the ground elder, and gave her seeds and cuttings. On moving to Northamptonshire, Rosy inherited the avenue which had very little growing behind its expanse of box hedging. '*Anemone japonica*, golden rod, and some clapped-out Michaelmas daisies – and a double white lilac.'

Over the years it has been filled with shrub roses, wisteria, and countless plants and cuttings from her mother. 'We have similar styles, we like the same plants.' There is now a continuous traffic of plants and advice and gardening gossip between them. 'We see each other whenever we can, we have a real rapport.'

Both have found the time to garden only at the expense of more conventional household routines. Children are sometimes forgotten. Rosy remembers 'demented fighting' with her brother and sister, whilst her mother blissfully gardened. Neither bothers with housework. Irene does it only when people come; Rosy not at all. Their domestic lives verge on the disastrous; taps over-run, food is burnt. As Rosy says,

> I put timers round my neck or in my pocket to remind me to take things out of the oven, but then I'd take off my jacket and get absorbed, and don't hear them. For a time my compost was filled with burnt bread.

Rosy does not think her sons are interested in gardening but her daughter Mary hovers and watches.

> She helps pick up the leaves. She makes potions from petals – she can distinguish the poisonous plants. She sorts the flowerpots in order. But she is a fairweather gardener. She won't come out if the weather is bad.

Who takes to gardening and when is unpredictable. Like most passions, it cannot be easily charted. When it does take hold, it is still sweeter if it is shared. If it has been shared for a long time, and across generations, the companionship and pleasure are amplified, and what is traditionally a close relationship, between mother and daughter, becomes still more valued. The mothers, daughters, and grand-daughters described in this chapter may well have their disagreements and bad patches, but their gardens draw them back into one another's lives.

CHAPTER FIVE

GOING WILD

John Parkinson, the seventeenth-century gardening expert, praised Mistress Thomasin Tunstall for scouting around in the woods and sending him a double cardamine and lady's slipper orchid. He thought other men and women should keep their eyes open for such rarities. 'Many things doe lye hid . . .' he wrote. For him, as for his contemporaries, nature was a source of riches, an unexplored largesse which needed tapping and utilizing. Taming nature, extracting from it new plants which could be used both for their beauty and their usefulness, was in his view the purpose of gardening.

Wild herbs and flowers offered all kinds of culinary and medicinal possibilities; flavourings, food decorations, remedies and poisons – from garlic, violets and feverfew to hemlock and wolf-bane. Learning how to identify these everyday plants growing naturally, how to cull and distil them, was part of the skill of being a good housewife. The distillery was an important room in the manor house, but even cottagers were likely to have some basic herbal lore.

This skill in identification of and reliance on natural resources may have been retained by rural housewives, but was soon lost sight of by the rich in favour of more highly cultivated fruit and vegetables. By the late eighteenth and nineteenth century, nature was being discovered all over again: this time in the interests of botany. The classification of British flora was a hobby for many genteel women, some of whom took it very seriously, as seriously as their

An informal combination of honeysuckle and geraniums at Kiftsgate Court in Gloucestershire.

status would allow them. They contributed to local censuses of plants, and gathered lichens, seaweed, ferns and fungi as well as flowers. For example, Mary Beever from the Lake District is recorded as supplying gentians and ferns to the Oxford Botanical Gardens; and Susan Beever, her sister, corresponded with John Ruskin. Miss Harriet Carlyon collected and drew the native British orchids in the Isle of Wight. There were many others, of whom there are brief passing references in the books of the time.

Some of these women wrote guides and notes for others. The most well known of these, Anne Pratt, was mentioned earlier. She attempted to write a complete guide to native plants, which was very popular. There were a number of other guides, often spoilt (or enhanced, depending on your temporal perspective) by sentimental and moral musings on the relationship between womanhood and unsullied nature. William Fitch, a botanical artist at Kew, was known outside horticultural circles as the illustrator of a book on native British flowers, which was a handbook for young ladies; they looked for the wild flowers and coloured in his pictures.

Nature was regarded as pure and innocent, and the undemanding study of native flora as a fitting hobby for young women. The purity of nature was also contrasted with the defiling atmosphere of the cities. The study of natural flora offered an antidote to the pollution and sordidness of the new industrial landscapes.

> With the enormous increase of our town populations there has grown up a truer appreciation of the country and of all that is beautiful in nature; and it is hoped that this work may be of service to those who thus steal back to the arms of their Mother,

wrote Edward Step, the author of *Wayside and Woodland Blossoms*, 1895, which offered a 'clear description of 394 species' for non-botanists.

Victorian gardens were highly ornate and stylized, and there was not much room for untidy nature within them. William Robinson's book *The Wild Garden*, first published in 1870, was another landmark. He argued that there was a place in the formal Victorian garden for nature and wild plants, although he considered that any plant which was perennial or self-sown, hardy, and could acclimatize itself in British gardens was 'natural' no matter where it came from.

He wanted gardens to look less regimented, and more informal; he begged his readers help him sound 'the death-note of the pastry-cook's garden' – as he described the typical Victorian garden.

Two of his contemporaries, Gertrude Jekyll and Mrs Earle, also thought more emphasis should be placed on informal settings and woodland scenes as part of a large garden. Gertrude Jekyll, in her dignified rhapsodic prose, considered that:

3. *Monopetalæ*   LIV. SOLANACEÆ   179

714. Hyoscyamus niger L.
Henbane; Y.

715. Solanum Dulcamara L.
Bittersweet, Nightshade; B.

716. Solanum nigrum L.
Black Nightshade.

717. Atropa Belladonna L.
Dwale, Deadly Nightshade; P

Illustrations by botanical artist Walter Hood from a book on British flora. Books like these were used for reference and as colouring-in books by generations of young ladies.

Beatrice Parsons

ABOVE
William Robinson who became a gardening guru for late-Victorian England. He hated Victorian bedding, and advocated the use of herbaceous plants and native English flowers rather than half-hardy annuals reared in glasshouses.

LEFT
A contemporary painting by Beatrice Parsons of William Robinson's wild garden. The wild garden was immaculately kept; wild did not mean abandoned.

> Wild gardening in any stretches of rough ground, or in woodland that may adjoin the garden, when practised with restraint and the most careful consideration, is, for true pleasure in beautiful effects, abundantly repaying.

They all held that nature was good to borrow from, and could be incorporated carefully as a backdrop for an artistic and well-kept garden.

As Jan Marsh in her book *Back to the Land* (1982) shows, people had ambivalent attitudes to the countryside. Rusticity was regarded as backward, if not despised. It was some of the socialist pioneers such as William Morris and Edward Carpenter who stressed the importance of rural values and living in harmony with nature – as opposed to sentimentalizing it or borrowing from it to make a civilized effect.

The two world wars changed our perceptions again, this time about the importance of the environment as a source of food. The Ministry of Health began systematic research into the drug value of native and cultivated herbs, and the National Federation of Women's Institutes, with its 6000 branches, was asked to help chart the availability and uses of natural flora. A National Herb Organizer, Dr R. A. Butcher, was appointed and worked through County Herb Committees. Elderflower cordial, rosehip syrup, hedgerow jam, nettle soup, dandelion coffee and mint tea, even sloe gin, reappeared in the recipe books. Mrs Florence Ranson wrote a best-selling paperback in the late 1940s entitled *British Herbs: a manual of herb recognition written for the layman and explaining to what uses native herbs can be put.*

As the days of austerity waned, this self-sufficiency gave way to Elizabeth David who opened our eyes to rich, perfectly cooked, gourmet food from France and Italy. Vegetarian food and do-it-yourself remedies were not merely unfashionable, they were for cranks and drop-outs. Nature was safeguarded by stricter planning regulations for the green belts surrounding cities, and in other protective legislation. The issues of cleaning up the towns and cities and preventing them from encroaching too much on the countryside were being addressed. We stopped worrying about nature.

In fact we were doing more damage to the natural environment than ever before, through modern agricultural practices. Farming subsidies made the clearance of marginal land profitable – hedges, woodlands, marshes, heaths and downlands were ploughed up. Natural habitats have disappeared at an alarming rate. Intensive stockrearing for meat and dairy consumption has meant that traditional grazing land has been turned over to intensive agriculture for stockfeed. The widespread use of nitrogenous fertilizers and herbicides draining into streams and rivers poisoned the waters. Agriculture has been extremely productive and efficient but at a terrible cost to the natural environment. In 1984 the Nature Conservancy Council reported that

> Ninety-five per cent of lowland grasslands and haymeadows lack any significant wild-life interest, and only 3 per cent are unaffected by agricultural improvement.

Nature can no longer be viewed as an inexhaustible retreat and native flora can no longer be taken for granted. The current emphasis is on conserving what remains; on guarding and regenerating a neglected aspect of our heritage. The enthusiasm for conservation, organic cultivation, urban wildlife, and green issues are part of the contemporary gardening scene. One of the most well-known and articulate spokeswomen for wild-life gardening is Miriam Rothschild, and her story highlights the general change in attitude.

> I garden purely for pleasure. I love plants and flowers and green leaves and I am incurably romantic – hankering after small stars spangling the grass.

Miriam Rothschild wrote this in *The Butterfly Gardener*, a book about her garden at Ashton Wold in Northamptonshire. She is formidable to write about, partly because her knowledge about plants and wildlife is scientific and empirical as well as passionately felt and has a rare depth and breadth; and partly because she writes with such erudition and wit herself.

She was born in 1908, a grand-daughter of the legendary Nathaniel Rothschild, banker and financial adviser to successive Victorian and Edwardian governments. She grew up partly in her grandfather's household at Tring, Hertfordshire. Her uncle Walter, a world famous and brilliant naturalist, also lived at home. He was exceedingly eccentric, a large, overweight and tongue-tied collector who founded Tring Museum, where he amassed hundreds of thousands of specimens of bird, mammal and entomological life, mainly skinned, stuffed and mounted, but some vigorously alive and roaming in the grounds of Tring Park. He was also a reluctant M.P. He was the leading representative of the Jewish community, and the Balfour declaration about the foundation of the state of Israel was addressed to him. Miriam Rothschild later wrote a biography of her uncle, entitled *Dear Lord Rothschild*. It has a photograph on the cover of him driving his carriage pulled by a team of zebras.

Miriam Rothschild's creeper-shrouded house at Ashton Wold. The effect of the dense, wild growth sometimes leads visitors to think the house is deserted.

Her father, Charles Rothschild, was also a naturalist, less flamboyant than his brother but also a diligent collector. He specialized in fleas and discovered the species which was the principal vector of bubonic plague. He stimulated Miriam Rothschild's own interest in fleas. (She is a world expert on the topic. There cannot be many people who rhapsodize about the capacities of the flea

but, after listening to Miriam Rothschild talk about cat fleas and their extraordinary jumping ability, and her efforts to measure how far and how often they leap, scientific enquiry takes on a new light.)

Charles Rothschild was one of the first to appreciate the need to conserve habitat rather than concentrating on preserving the rare species themselves. He founded the Society for the Promotion of Nature Reserves in 1912. The Society, alarmed at the way in which land was being ploughed up for wartime production, tried to identify a list of potential nature reserves as wildlife habitats. This was the forerunner of the Nature Conservancy Council and Sites of Special Scientific Interest (SSSIs).

Miriam Rothschild's inheritance was in every way remarkable. She was steeped in ideas about conservation, as she describes it, 'a mixture of science, curiosity and emotional involvement'. She also inherited Ashton Wold from her father. This comprised the family residence, a large farm, a model Edwardian thatched village and a woodland nature reserve.

In her father's day there were 14 gardeners looking after the extensive gardens; herbaceous and rose borders, an iris collection later donated to Kew, walled kitchen and fruit gardens, and glasshouses in which he raised orchids, cacti, creepers, and blue water-lilies from Lake Victoria in Africa. It was a classical Edwardian garden.

Her father died in 1923. The collections of botanical interest were dispersed. Her mother continued to maintain the garden; she was particularly fond of her avenue of hybrid tea roses and of violas.

Meanwhile, Miriam Rothschild was leading her own life. Although she had no formal scientific qualifications, she worked as a marine biologist studying Tematode worms at the Marine Biological Laboratories in Plymouth and Naples. The laboratories were bombed in the Blitz, putting an end to the research; and her mother died. She returned to Ashton Wold to look after the farm and gardens, qualified as a dairymaid and as an air raid warden, and married. She went to work at the Foreign Office for a short time.

She settled down at Ashton and had six children, but she maintained her research interests. In the evenings she studied with a microscope – microscopy being a magical diversion from the pressures of domesticity.

Her mother's gardener Charles Wright had also died, and John Stanton who succeeded him was a brilliant plantsman who delighted in horticultural shows and displays. He won R.H.S. gold medals for flowers, vegetables and fruit. But during the war the conventional bedding and herbaceous borders had been abandoned, and the alpines and water plants were overgrown or lost by neglect. Miriam Rothschild planted wild cherry trees, and bulbs in the grass. The water garden was left to the water-lilies.

She moved to Oxford, and Ashton became a weekend home. It was only in 1970, when in her sixties, that she moved back to Ashton Wold for good. Her son rebuilt the house, took the top floor off, and lowered the roof, changing the style from baronial hall to manor house. It was at that point she started rethinking the garden.

By then she had fewer staff, and the glasshouses were falling into disrepair. She could not maintain the garden as it had been in its heyday. Her tastes and feelings about the garden had changed too.

> I have always been passionately fond of wild flowers – when I was four years old my greatest thrill was finding white violets in the ditches and hedgerows . . . Then I grew to love cultivated flowers, and when I was in my teens I thought the most wonderful flowers in the world were cattleyas. I loved growing flamboyant flowers, especially water-lilies. I was crazy about water-lilies. Eventually I returned to my first love and settled down to grow buttercups and daisies.

Miriam Rothschild was appalled at the changes that had taken place around Ashton, the loss of native flora from fields and road verges, due to agricultural practices and road maintenance programmes. She decided to concentrate on wild flowers, for herself, and to stimulate interest in conservation.

The house at Ashton had been reduced in size by her son so she replanted the area immediately around the rebuilt house. In the front of the house overlooking the garden she planted a mixture of wild and cultivated climbers; ivies and virginia creeper, wild roses and ramblers, honeysuckles, the native *Clematis vitalba*, laburnum, plums and quince, and a white buddleia which grew 15 feet, so that she could watch from her bedroom window a cloud of butterflies nectaring from the blooms. In the courtyard by the entrance to the house she has slung ropes to carry vigorous cultivated climbing roses, such as

Miriam Rothschild celebrating her wild flowers. The site was originally a tennis court, and the flowers are the outcome of 10 years' systematic experimentation with the germination and propagation of native plants.

Rosa filipes 'Kiftsgate'. Even obtaining natural coloured rope was a problem as most thick rope contains blue dye. The house is so covered with plants that visitors wonder if anyone really lives in this sleeping beauty tangle of greenery.

Recreating a personal vision of beauty was not enough. Miriam Rothschild was deeply concerned about conservation. She had been a member of the executive committee of the Society for the Promotion of Nature Reserves (S.P.N.R.) for 30 years but realized she knew nothing about growing wild flowers. She began by allowing the grass of three-quarters of an acre of tennis courts and croquet lawns to grow naturally into a mini-hayfield. She collected seeds of wild flowers from a derelict airfield close by and planted them in these lawns. She was pleasantly surprised at the result. She attended a lecture by Professor Melanby at Cambridge, who said that it would take a thousand years to recreate a mediaeval flowering hayfield. With typical confidence and panache, she suggested she could produce a very good imitation in ten.

As a scientist, she experimented systematically with growing wild flowers. In the kitchen garden she planted long rows of single species, as if they were radishes or peas, and built up a seed bank. A number of seedlings of cowslips, ox-eye daisies, harebells, violets or vetches and knapweed from this source were introduced into the lawns and grass banks. For annuals she developed her 'farmer's nightmare' mixture of cornflowers, corncockle, corn marigold, poppies and mayweed – the weeds that farmers had for centuries tried to eliminate.

The tennis court lawn worked; its rubbly base was a good habitat for the wild flowers she wanted to encourage. After ten years, wild orchids arrived – 'they came in from the cold' – the bee orchid, the twayblade, pyramidal and spotted orchid. Other plants appeared, and by the fifteenth year there were 90 species of flowering plants and grasses. The cowslips had also multiplied, and in the spring of 1991 it was estimated that there were about 10,000 plants in bloom – a golden carpet. The patterning of the flowers varies according to the season and the micro-climates; by June, the cowslips have gone but there are denser patches of the native British geranium, the mauve-blue cranesbill; in other patches, yellows or reds of vetches and knapweed predominate. Buttercups are scattered through the meadow; ox-eye daisies grow in profusion and move gently in the breezes. Bright blue chicory and pink restharrow (*Ononis repens*) grow side by side. The delicate spikes of the orchids are scattered through the grasses. Butterflies, moths, bees and other insects flutter and hum through the flowers.

Around the house there were other changes. The creepers and climbers hide the house. Many bulbs were planted in the grass banks which separate the house and lawn from the tennis court – tulips, crocus, jonquils, alliums. There are also martagon lilies; and irises – blue, white and pale mauve – rise through the grasses. Separating the bank from the field, there are a variety of native trees, crab apples, plums, pears. Stone steps overgrown with valerian and lady's bedstraw (*Galium verum*) lead down into the meadow. Immediately outside the house there is a long straight gravel path running along its length, bordered with the native scarlet wild poppy, mayweed, cornflowers, corncockle and other annuals from the farmer's nightmare mixture.

The woods on the estate were established in her father's time and have been carefully managed ever since. The elms have gone, but there are avenues of chestnuts, and new trees are planted every year. The bird population has been undisturbed for 100 years and although they sometimes decimate the blossom and fruit trees their existence is precious – even the flowers must 'make-do'. Miriam Rothschild listens to birds singing and speculates on their intentions.

> I have a passion for robins singing in the rain. I believe their songs to be outbursts of beautiful rage.

Her greatest accolade came from a Northamptonshire neighbour, the late Sir David Scott. He was a very great plantsman, and cultivated or introduced many rare plants and shrubs. He visited Ashton Wold.

> He happened to come on a day when it was looking at its best in the spring, and he stood on my lawn, and he said this is the prettiest garden I've ever seen. And I really felt crowned, you know.

The success in the garden encouraged her to attempt the recreation of flowering hayfields on a larger scale. She extended the experimentation to 52 acres of farmland. She realized how little was known about the pollination, germination, growth and dispersal of wild flower populations. It was very hard work. What sort of seed bed was required? Italian rye grass? Leys? Turf? Bare

The glasshouse originally housed tropical water-lilies, including a giant Victoria lily. Now, unheated and slightly cracked, it is given over to native British water-lilies, which Miriam Rothschild considers amongst the most beautiful of all plants.

soil? Stubble? How should one sow the seed? Broadcast by hand, or drill, or harrow? How should one collect the seed? By hand? With a vacuum cleaner? Should one cut the field all at once, or stagger the harvest so as to collect both early and late seed ripeners? Should fields be grazed after harvest? One particular species fascinated her. Yellow rattle (*Rhinanthus minor*) is a semi-parasite of grass and reduces the growth of grasses giving broadleaved flowers a better chance to flourish. But its germinating process is very unusual and seeds will not germinate in spring, only in autumn, although no one knows how or why.

The scale of these activities was very different from that of her garden, and the experimentation was more scientifically controlled. This too was successful, and the possibilities it raised for preserving native flora were widely acknowledged. She has been awarded the Victoria Medal of Honour, like her grandfather before her. Both the National Trust and the R.H.S. have now begun to adopt, in part at least, an interest in wild flowers. Many of the big country landowners are also turning over parts of their estates to wild flower conservation, under the Ministry of Agriculture set-aside scheme. Some of the counties are also actively experimenting with roadside schemes, replanting verges, and delaying cutting them, in order to let the flowers seed.

Along with propagation and distribution has been publicity for the conservation cause. This has included Miriam Rothschild's book, *The Butterfly Gardener*, a television programme with Ladybird Johnson about roadside verges in Texas and in Britain; and generally using her influence and connections in the scientific world and in society to advocate wild flower gardening. This has led to some valuable (in conservation rather than financial terms) commissions, such as the planting of the swards at Stanstead Airport.

Miriam Rothchild's 'Farmer's Nightmare' seed mix planted at Chatsworth.

Her latest project has been the conversion of a disused airfield into a wild rose garden, part of an ambition to see the hedgerows of England festooned with wild roses. The land belonged to the estate, but was requisitioned by the government for use by bombers during the war, and honeycombed with underground tunnels which were once rocket sites. Four varieties of wild rose have been encouraged to seed themselves and the whole area is now covered with gentle foaming pink and white roses. Cinquefoils and other small creeping flowers push through the cracks in the concrete. The only sound is from the birdsong; nightingales breed there. It is utterly quiet and eerily beautiful. About 4000 cuttings are collected each autumn and transferred into the kitchen garden to be grown into bushes.

Miriam Rothschild is now in her eighties but, in her own words, 'tough as old boots'. Her energy and enthusiasm are undiminished. She is a self-declared eccentric. 'I've never really cared what other people think or say – isn't that a definition of eccentricity?' She has always gone her own way, refusing to let her creativity and intellect be trammelled by anyone else's rules – to the benefit of science. She is happily wilful, chuckling at past disputes. She spends what spare time she has watching the sport on Sky television, and says she has been a sports addict all her life. It is difficult to do justice to her originality and the stimulus of her company. Wild flower gardening has had in her an extraordinary champion.

The wildlife movement has become popular. As Miriam Rothschild pointed out, she lent a voice and a practical impetus to a movement that already existed. Ironically, the idea of natural habitats for wildlife is almost as popular in the cities as in the countryside; in some ways the cities have become greener than the polluted countryside. As well as the individuals who choose to make part or all of their gardens a haven for wildlife, there are numerous small organizations dedicated to preserving wildlife habitats in urban areas. These are often run collectively, employing ecologists, botanists and environmental scientists, and using local volunteers.

The London Wildlife Garden Centre in the borough of Southwark was created from an old council depot located behind late nineteenth-century, terraced, working-class housing. It has attracted much publicity and many local visitors. The group who run it created a variety of habitats on the site, including a hay meadow, a hedgerow, a pond and marshy areas with wild flower borders. The centre also functions as a tree and wild flower nursery, with demonstration organic compost heaps.

The centre's aim is 'to involve as many people as possible regardless of age, ability or experience'. It certainly attracts people who have had no interest or knowledge of the gardening circles represented by the R.H.S. The oldest volunteer, who is eighty and is to be seen regularly working on the site, was once a road-worker based in the depot. Elderly local shoppers drop by to sit on a bench and admire the honeysuckle and the wild roses. There is a turf-roofed wooden building which is used as a study centre by schools, including a local school for those with learning difficulties. Various clubs, such as the South London Organic Gardeners' Group, a local group of the Henry Doubleday Research Association, meet at the centre. The Wildlife Centre also organizes regular events throughout spring and summer, walks, workshops, water surveys and a local wildlife festival.

There are community gardens, wildlife parks and sites in many of our cities. These are a break from gardening tradition, collective rather than individual, run on egalitarian and co-operative lines, free and accessible, and dedicated to raising consciousness about the importance of conservation and natural habitats. The organizations who conserve and maintain them see gardening as a public rather than a private activity, and their intervention is as much political (to draw attention to the plight of the environment) as in the interests of art or design, or plants and horticulture, or any of the traditional interests and obsessions of gardening. Perhaps it is an injustice to suppose that beauty and layout are unimportant and style is irrelevant in these city gardens. The elderly shoppers might not be as articulate as Miriam Rothschild; and a depot surrounded by terraced housing is a more restricted site than the Northamptonshire countryside; but they may well share her sentiment that natural beauty is too precious to lose:

> . . . as the summer wears on and the stems and leaves turn a light beige in colour, the pale mauve cranesbill, half-hidden dreamily in the straw-coloured bent grasses, seem infinitely more beautiful to me than any flower in well-weeded bed.

HIGH STYLE

What is a garden for? For the very rich in the seventeenth and eighteenth centuries, it was an expression of wealth and power; a way of showing that nature itself could be ordered and reconceived. For the less wealthy it was a food store, a collection of herbs, vegetables and fruit, on which the family's well-being depended. In Victorian times it became a display case for exotica.

By contrast today, when children and leisure have pride of place, a garden is often viewed as an outside 'rumpus room', a place where young children can splash and dig and ride bikes, somewhere to play ball games or practise golf shots, a space to hang the washing. Or else it is an outside dining room, a place to barbecue, to sit and talk and sip white wine or lemonade or tea, despite the weather. The floral accompaniments to these activities are usually bright, reliable, maintenance free, and hopefully cheap, like posters pinned to a wall to liven up a room. It is often the activities which go on in it rather than the garden itself which come first.

These robust views about gardening are one end of a continuum. At the other end are those that see gardening as a fine art, a matter of 'good taste' and of an education which has included familiarity with the grand manners and gardens of the past, especially those in France and Italy; and whose own gardens contain at least faint echoes of other epochs.

Somewhere near this end of the range is the view that gardening is fashion;

The knot garden at Barnsley House,
its pattern accentuated by snow.

a first cousin of interior decoration, a composition of plants and garden furniture, akin to the furnishings of a house, carefully colourful, clever and usually expensive. It encapsulates romantic visions of the countryside, away from the rush and restrictions of urban life. This idealized romantic garden does not lend itself to rough play. Lawns and bikes are not compatible; children are elsewhere.

One of the most well-known contemporary garden designers is Rosemary Verey. For nine years she wrote a monthly article, 'The Country Woman's Notes', for the magazine *Country Life*, and she is the author of a number of best-selling gardening books. She has been featured in *Vogue*, the *Field*, *House and Garden*, the *Connoisseur*, and the colour supplements of various Sunday newspapers, and in 1989 she won the Christie's and Historic Houses Association Garden of the Year Award. She is frequently asked to lecture in America.

Barnsley House, her husband David's family-home in Gloucestershire, is a seventeenth-century mellowed stone mansion, and here she and David have slowly made a garden in the four acres around it. Rosemary Verey has written about how and why she took up gardening. She stayed at home to bring up her family of four. 'A happy country life, ponies, tennis, that sort of thing.' Although her sons went to prep school when they were eight and later to Eton, she educated her two daughters at home until the age of 11. She found teaching them a fruitful activity, and sees in this the roots of her interest in writing.

> I enjoy talking to people about gardening, the pleasures of gardening, the visual things. The experience [of teaching my daughters] forced me into putting words together, and I enjoy writing, I enjoy saying what I feel and think . . . sitting in the garden, and thinking, well it's beautiful and I'd like to explain it.

Once her children were older, her attention turned to gardening. She went to see other people's gardens, read, both old and contemporary books, and kept copious notes.

> I'm not a person who does things by halves. If I do a thing I like to do it well and work hard at it.

She gradually accumulated a library of rare books, 'collecting herbals before it was fashionable to do so'. These books were a source of ideas and inspiration. Other influences included John Raven, Vita Sackville-West, Russell Page, and Nancy Lindsay, whom she visited often and whose garden impressed her, 'just paths and plants . . . I went more in winter than in summer, she had wonderful hellebores, foliage and ferns'.

She admired the garden rooms of Sissinghurst and Hidcote, but felt they would not suit her terrain or her developing ideas.

> I felt that Barnsley, with its surrounding stone wall and house neatly set in the middle, should not have a series of enclosures but rather a series of areas defined by pathways leading to new enclosures.

She started at the drawing-room door, leading over a terrace to a Cotswold stone path flanked by Irish yews, where she sowed rock rose seeds. In 1964 the 10-year-old lime walk was extended into a laburnum avenue underplanted with alliums, ending in a fountain against the wall. By 1971 she was exhibiting plants at the R.H.S. show. In 1975 the knot-garden was made, then the vegetable garden, which lay outside the boundaries of the main walled garden. In 1964 her husband, an architectural historian working for the Ministry of Housing on listed buildings, was allowed to take and restore a derelict eighteenth-century temple from neighbouring Fairford Park, which became the focus of the pool garden. The garden evolved, and Rosemary Verey says that in retrospect the temple 'puts a construction on it that wasn't there'. She describes her gardening as reflective, 'When you feel uncertain it's particularly important to stand and stare.'

She likes the idea of alleys, vistas, box hedges, patterns and knot-gardens. This formality, heightened by carefully placed sculptures and garden furniture, and softened by pretty planting, mostly in muted colours, are the characteristics of her style. Her patterned vegetable garden in particular has attracted both admiration and ridicule: admiration for its innovation and clever use of the decorative features of fruit and vegetables; and ridicule that growing fruit and vegetables should have so little to do with cooking and eating them. Although, in fact, the vegetable garden is highly productive, providing the family and other people with vegetables all through the year. There are no alpines, 'I am not good with little things', and few rhododendrons, or bedding plants. She describes her style as a contemporary one, combining the best of informal cottage garden planting within a formal framework. It is this style, easily identifiable, which has been so plagiarized by other garden designers and, in the words of one gardening journalist, became 'the look of the 1980s'.

Her garden requires intensive upkeep, clipping, cutting back, weeding, replanting. She does not use groundcover as such but dislikes bare earth, so a constant succession of plants is required to give the effect she seeks. One of her earliest and most prized garden possessions is her propagating equipment, and she enjoys being able to sell the extra plants she grows. These days her literary output and her garden commissions leave her little time to work in the

garden herself. Now in her seventies, she discusses with her two full-time gardeners and various helpers the work that needs to be undertaken.

Her writing grew out of her gardening, trying to explain to a wider audience how she had made her garden. She wrote her first article for the *Countryman*, and then walked into the editor's office to ask whether he would take it. Her first book, *The Englishwoman's Garden*, which garden designer Alvilda Lees-Milne asked her to co-edit, featured a series of women garden owners writing about their gardens, lavishly illustrated with lush photographs. The gardens belonged to 'all the people we knew', mainly titled or wealthy women. The formula was a success, repeated in *The New Englishwoman's Garden*, *The Englishman's Garden*, *The American Woman's Garden* and so on – five titles so far.

LEFT
Clever planting of alliums and polygonums at Barnsley House.

ABOVE
Rosemary Verey standing in the town garden she designed for the Chelsea Flower Show in 1992.

Other books followed at a prolific rate; *Good Planting, The Scented Garden, Classic Garden Design, The Garden in Winter, The Flower Arranger's Garden*, and a reissue in book form of her *Countrywoman's Notes*. The books display her wide reading, her knowledge of plants, and her conviction that she has a mission to explain beauty. More books are in the pipeline, a formidable output.

In 1992 Rosemary Verey was asked to design a town garden for the *Evening Standard* at the Chelsea Flower Show. The logistics of any Chelsea exhibit are demanding, a garden even more so. Her solution to the small space available was to miniaturize: tiny box hedges, a tiny vegetable plot with a handful of ornamental vegetables, a tiny octagonal lawn with a pretty border – a doll's-house garden. This illustrated both the strengths and weaknesses of her approach: the combination of formality and prettiness; and the difficulties in adapting or generalizing beyond a style derived for country houses. As she herself commented, 'You are influenced by the social milieu in which you live.' Interviewed on the television programme *Gardeners' World* about her garden for Chelsea, she was asked about a particular lemon verbena shrub shaped as a standard which stood in one corner. 'Shh,' she replied, 'I borrowed it from Prince Charles's conservatory, but don't tell him because he doesn't know yet.'

Another influential gardening writer and designer is Penelope Hobhouse. Like Rosemary Verey she is self-taught and of a similar social background. After going to Cambridge University, she married and started gardening, first in a farm garden. 'I suddenly realized gardening was a sort of art form.' She had little idea of what she was doing, but rushed off to buy plants. She visited her Somerset neighbour Margery Fish, and, in her initial ignorance, took for granted the extraordinary range of plants in her nursery. Garden experts and writers John and Faith Raven gave her advice. She had family connections with Knightshayes (the Devon garden created by the Amory family, and now in the hands of the National Trust), and felt stimulated by its creative approach to gardening, and the superb range of its plants. All her surplus energy was spent in gardening.

She and her husband then moved to Hadspen House and its seven-acre garden. This had been well laid-out but it had become overrun with weeds. Penelope Hobhouse struggled to clear and replant it and, because of the shortage of labour on the large estate, she focused on ground cover and low-maintenance planting. In the process of restoration, she became interested in garden design and started to visit gardens abroad. She also began her first book, *The Country Gardener*. This is a workmanlike and practical book which opens with an apology.

> As I am only an amateur gardener, with no professional, horticultural or botanical background or training, it may seem presumptuous of me . . . to write a book about country gardening.

Despite the satisfactions of gardening and writing she eventually left her husband and Hadspen and persuaded the National Trust to take her on as a tenant for the Tintinhull garden in Somerset. Tintinhull is one of their most graceful properties, donated to the Trust by Phyllis Reiss. She moved there in 1979 with John Malins, later her second husband, who died in 1992. The upheaval was both disturbing and exhilarating.

> I really vowed to myself I would never be dependent on a man again, so I had to work. And that's a great spur and actually if you start earning so late in life it's intoxicating . . . I still get enormous pleasure for being paid for what I do, because for so long I didn't work and felt rather useless, I was just a wife and mother, and yet . . . they made you feel [at Cambridge] that you should be doing something good and useful besides having children.

The fact that Penelope Hobhouse is now a professional working woman, with a formidable daily timetable, is sometimes hard for her friends and acquaintances to understand.

> Now I have a completely separate career . . . it has moved me into a different world . . . at first I worked in the garden sixty hours a week, and wrote the books as a sideline. I was so happy.

Maintaining Tintinhull has not been without its problems. When the National Trust took it over, there was a complete inventory of the plants in the garden, and it was not clear to Penelope Hobhouse how much leeway would be allowed for any new planting, or how much the original planting would have to be followed to the letter. As always, some old favourites died, others became more rampant, new varieties of plants came on the market, and it was with some unease she felt obliged to maintain the status quo. Eventually she decided, because of the intimate character of the garden, and the ephemerality of gardening, she would take upon herself the role of interpreter.

> I knew Mrs Reiss . . . she had no access to these plants . . . we pretend she would have chosen them. We behave as if she was alive and experimenting.

The next milestone was a commission to write the book, *Colour in Your Garden*. This profoundly influenced her thinking and made her name.

> It actually changed my life because for two years I thought of nothing but colour . . . I looked at more and more Impressionists to see what they were trying to do. I read books about colour theory . . . it became a sort of obsession . . . I saw things in the landscape that I'd never noticed before . . . the different colours you've got, if you saw shadows when there was snow on the ground and the greens and pinks that you got as a reflection from green.

The book was beautifully illustrated with photographs and published to much acclaim. Many gardeners cite it as a key reference. As Penelope Hobhouse's fame grew, more commissions arrived, and more visitors arrived at Tintinhull. Although the garden is not open daily, there are many group appointments, and in May and June visitors come every day including Sundays. This is an exhausting schedule.

> Actually we only have one ticket lady and we had to get a steward to stand in here and in the end I am a substitute for everybody . . . I'm a substitute for my daily when she goes on holiday, so I clean the public lavatories . . . and I'm taking the tickets because my wonderful Jean has to have some time off. And I'm trying to write and garden . . . in the end it is becoming too much.

Penelope Hobhouse,
head gardener at Tintinhull.

There is inevitable conflict between running a garden which is open to the public, and a personal need for privacy, and wanting to get on with the tasks which need doing. She can be seen busy about her garden jobs by visitors to the garden, her hair slightly dishevelled, wearing working clothes with a stout gardener's apron, the skin on her hands cracked from constant contact with the soil.

> I get a bit claustrophobic when the public walk through the house . . . I get more and more glowery . . . I have to conquer my feelings.

Through Tintinhull and through her publications, in particular, *Colour in Your Garden* and her scholarly *Garden Style*, Penelope Hobhouse attracted American commissions and has visited America frequently. Her visits to American clients are stimulating but often frenetic, and she has found herself travelling long distances, with little time to reflect. She feels the commissions give her a chance to create:

> I'm in it to make money but it's one's duty to leave something beautiful behind . . . I'm an instinctive designer who's learnt from history and worked by memory of what I've seen and adapted . . . I only really like using real stone and slate and those things but it's partly ignorance, I'd love to have done a proper training.

Sometimes she faces a difficult client.

> I can't communicate the vision . . . I'd be mad to fall out . . . I've got to make them think their garden beautiful when I've finished, so it's up to me.

She regrets there is so little overlap between public and private gardens in England, and that no commissions come for designing and planting public gardens, where she feels her social connections and glossy publications are seen as something of a handicap, 'They lap it up in America but in this country it's a disadvantage.' She cites the Conservatory garden in Central Park, New York as an example of what she would like to do. It is funded both privately and publicly, it is a widely admired design, and is a resource for Fifth Avenue matrons and downtown Harlem alike, a social mix that is rarely paralleled in England.

Focus on garden style and garden design, and an emphasis on the structure and overall composition of the garden, is a widespread preoccupation, and not confined to those with large gardens, or to rich Americans. The Society of Garden Designers has been set up as a self-regulatory body to promote the profession of garden design and to guarantee standards. Elizabeth Whately is a typical member. She was a domestic science mistress at a local school for many years, but became increasingly interested in gardening as a hobby, and went on various gardening courses. She took redundancy in her fifties, and trained with John Brookes, the internationally-known garden designer based in Sussex. She then set up in business on her own. She has had to learn the basics of surveying, producing estimates, drawing up plans, putting plans out to tender, overseeing contractors, familiarizing herself with wholesale nurseries, and promoting her design work.

She mainly works on a small scale with customers who are new to gardening. She issues a sheet to all prospective customers outlining what her work will involve, and on what kind of basis she can be hired. The unwritten part of her job is to offer a crash course in gardening to her clients, who may know very little about the care and maintenance of the plants they select. Often the clients do not think of the garden as a living, growing entity, but as an interior, a fixed entity. She makes compromises between what she thinks looks good and what the client wants and can afford.

> In the end it's what makes the client happy. I may not like what they choose, but they are paying for it, and they have to live with it and I do the best I can.

The tension is there for all garden designers between their own views about garden style and what clients choose. Some designers will not take on commissions if conflict is likely; others suppress their own views; most negotiate. Getting one's work known without social or gardening connections is difficult. Marketing is as important as garden credentials: brochures, advertising, appearing at shows and so on. Many clients do not realize what work is involved in giving advice, and ask for free tips, or give inadequate details. 'You do not say how cold it is,' wrote Graham Stuart Thomas to one anxious inquirer. 'Have a good look around the district and see what is successful.'

Garden journalism influences how people think about their gardens. A generation ago, most of the gardening correspondents for national papers and monthly magazines, and the editors of the gardening journals were men (although the *Observer* did employ Vita Sackville-West and Frances Perry, and Anne Scott-James was a regular contributor to the radio programme *Gardeners' Question Time*). Much of the advice they gave was ruminative and practical, with hints and tips about making gardens more productive and keeping weeds and

ABOVE
The self-seeding nigella is used generously at Tintinhull. Here it is grouped with yellow iris and *Allium albopilosum*.

RIGHT
A beautifully constructed vista looking back towards the yellow Ham-stone manor house.

pests at bay, although there would be occasional articles about gardens and nurseries. Now, women predominate as columnists; Mary Keen, Ursula Buchan, Miranda Innes, Francesca Greenoak all have regular columns. Whether or not it is a more feminine approach, a sign of the individualistic times, or merely due to the availability of higher quality photographs in the Sunday supplements, individual gardens and gardeners are increasingly being featured more often.

Anna Pavord, the gardening journalist, at her 300-year-old Dorsetshire cottage. Her time at the cottage represents only a fraction of its history; she resists notions of 'proprietorial ownership'.

One of the most influential of the columnists, although she modestly refutes it, is Anna Pavord. She describes herself as a 'hack', a feature journalist who was given the 'gift' of a gardening column in the *Independent* newspaper, on the strength of a one-off article she had written about gardening in another paper. She feels strongly that it is not her job to arbitrate on questions of taste and style, but to give a sense of the idiosyncrasies and passions involved in gardening.

> I'm an anarchist . . . I believe gardening is about creating your own little world . . . I want to encourage people to believe in their own convictions, to have the strength to go their own way.

She has an eclectic approach towards gardens. She does not mind whether people grow 'unfashionable' flowers such as marigolds, begonias or exhibition chrysanthemums; she does not care what colours are placed next to each other – pinks, oranges and yellows, bright blues and reds. These are individual preferences and there are no rights and wrongs. But she does care that plants should be grown well, whatever they are. She regards a good garden as:

... the creation of something that satisfies the soul ... somehow everything as it should be ... a kind of balance ... You don't know what it is until you see it, it's a physical manifestation of the love put into it, a radiance in the plants ... which you can find equally well in a garden 10 foot square or in the huge grounds of a country house.

She explains the popularity of gardening as 'a kind of restorative process'. Her television series *Flowering Passions* tapped the ways in which ordinary people approach gardening. Some like digging, some like the mathematical precision of pruning, some like nursing the plants – even to the extent of getting up at three in the morning to check the temperature in the greenhouse. The result is 'brilliantly grown plants' from people who have observed closely and care about what they grow.

Anna Pavord stresses that she is not an expert herself and, although she lives and gardens in the country, tries to resist any notion of 'proprietorial ownership'. Her house and garden are over 300 years old, so her residence there will never be more than a temporary phase in the life of the garden. Some of the old structures in the garden have been restored, some new trees planted, but she regards herself as 'passing through'.

This eclectic approach, the accent on individuality, and the denial of the importance of traditional ideas about design, is a populist one. It contradicts the view that the history of garden design and style is about the grand gardens of the very rich. The urge to decorate, the need to elaborate one's environment is a basic one. 'Diversity and ornamentation', wrote the biologist Stephen Jay Gould, are what make humans tick. Herbert Read, the art historian, also argues that, 'the object in making the work of art is ... the thoroughly human, everyday aim of "brightening things up a bit" '.

Russell Page, the garden designer whose book *The Education of a Gardener* (1962) is a gardening landmark, argued that style transcends time and place; that it is a humanizing vision.

If the garden designer is an artist ... it [is] his business to observe life and people; he must try to understand them and select from and transmute his experience first into design and then into reality.

CHAPTER SEVEN

FLOWERS AND FOLIAGE

Flowers and gardens have inspired many great artists. 'If you can paint one leaf,' wrote art critic John Ruskin, 'you can paint the world.' Albrecht Dürer's sixteenth-century watercolours of the iris and of meadow turf; the sumptuous bouquets of seventeenth-century Dutch painters; Van Gogh's sunflowers and Monet's lilies; the forms and colours of flowers and foliage have always excited artistic imagination. Painting flowers has also been part of scientific enquiry, a means of describing and noting botanical discoveries, and logging the extraordinary diversity of the plant kingdom. The discovery of plants was once a frontier science; like bio-genetics or astronomy today, it was once a source of wonder, delight and endless speculation. Accurate drawings of the plant discoveries were an essential part of the process of exploration and acquisition.

Meticulously recording the individuality of plants was one aspect of botanical art; beauty played a part too. The artists displayed sheer delight in the visual and painterly qualities of their subjects. Botanical art was a way of seeing, and the way in which plants were portrayed became a special trade of its own, whose exponents have become justly famous, Pierre-Joseph Redouté (the nineteenth-century flower painter) most of all. His paintings of

An unknown artist sketching poppies
at Chelsea Physic Garden.

Rosa rapa by
Redouté. He was
the most
fashionable of all
flower painters. His
patron was the
Empress Josephine,
and his pupils
included most of
the ladies of the
Parisian aristocracy.

roses and lilies are not only accurate in every detail, with a subtle sense of
perspective, they are also sensuous, exquisite and resplendent, recording the
Empire's flowers. His contemporary, Goethe, argued that botanical art was
more challenging and rewarding than any other form of painting:

> The one had only to satisfy the lover of superficial beauty; the other has to
> give truth – and through truth, beauty.

As with all art forms, creativity, talent and inspired observation are not enough
to make a name. Botanical art depended on commissions, patronage and
ultimately on the value society ascribed to the work. As the science of botany
became more important and more fashionable, the patronage grew. The
famous sixteenth-century printing house of Plantin in Antwerp supported a
gallery of artists, which led to a revival of botanical drawing. The Empress
Josephine was Redouté's patron, and her bountiful allowance helped set him
up. When it ceased he became bankrupt. In Britain, the Duchess of Beaufort
commissioned Everhardus Kickius in 1703 to paint the plants grown at
Badminton in Avon; and half a century later the Duchess of Portland

encouraged and generously paid Georg Ehret to paint flowers at Bulstrode in Buckinghamshire, paintings as beautiful and as accurate as those of Redouté.

In Holland, which had more enlightened attitudes towards women in the seventeenth and eighteenth centuries, women artists were allowed to join the guilds, to have their own studios, and seek commissions on a professional basis. The emphasis was as much on flowers for art's sake as on flowers for science's sake, and the paintings were sometimes cheaper to buy than the flowers they portrayed. Maria van Oosterwyk and Rachel Ruysch were the most well-known of the independent and self-assured women artists. They produced brilliant still-lives of flowers and fruit; soft, clear and flawless. Maria Merian was a botanist and entomologist, and many of her lucid drawings were made during a trip she made in 1698, at the age of 53, to Surinam. In Paris, Madeleine de Basseporte took over the office of the great French botanical artist, Aubriet, in 1735, and produced the botanical illustrations for the *Jardin du Roi*; her friend Anne Vallayer Coster was noted for her paintings of flowers.

By contrast, women artists of the period in Britain were producing pretty

Mrs Delany, a friend of the Duchess of Portland and a skilled artist, who specialized in paper cut-outs of flowers. She was best-known to her contemporaries for her good manners.

miniatures. Mrs Delany, the Duchess of Portland's close friend, was making paper cut-outs of flowers, and was respected not so much because of her eye for colour, or her dexterity with scissors, but for her feminine virtues. Dr Johnson wrote of her, 'she was the highest bred woman in the world and the woman of fashion of all ages'. Her own expectations, and the expectations held of her, could not have been more different from those of her co-resident at Portland, Georg Ehret. Mary Moser was a founder member of the Royal Academy in 1768 but, although she exhibited regularly, and her flower bouquets are pretty, she laid no claims to botany. Only Elizabeth Blackwell, mentioned earlier as the author of *A Curious Herbal*, bucked the trend, but she was an odd exception, and produced nothing else.

Botanizing – recognizing and drawing flowers – was a hobby for women in eighteenth- and nineteenth-century England, and practised as part of a range of accomplishments essential to good breeding, including playing a musical instrument, embroidery and dancing. Wilfrid Blunt, ex-drawing master at Eton (and who, according to one distinguished visitor to his home, planted plastic flowers in the tubs outside his front door), has written the authoritative standard reference on the history of botanical drawing, *The Art of Botanical Illustration*. He is unsympathetic in his treatment of women and considers their efforts to be generally trivial, at least until this century.

> The Linnaean system of classification . . . converted botany into a parlour game for any young lady who could count up to twelve.

Germaine Greer in her book *The Obstacle Race* also commented on the way watercolour paintings of flowers were trivialized as a woman's pursuit.

> Flowers were chosen as a fit subject for people who were not meant to take their artistic activity too seriously, and commercially manufactured paper, pencils and watercolours were not smelly or messy or in any way unfeminine.

The story of Elizabeth Twining (1805–89), from the famous tea merchant family, was typical. She sketched and painted in watercolours, and had a lifelong interest in botany. For many years she was occupied in preparing a botanical work entitled *Illustrations of the Natural Orders of Plants*. Like her

Elizabeth Twining was a competent botanist and a charming painter. But her true memorial, according to one commentator, was 'the Mothers' Meeting'.

contemporaries, she also published religious tracts, and it is for these, rather than for her botanical drawings, by which she is remembered. Blunt did not think highly of her talent, and wrote of her, 'Her true memorial is the Mothers' Meeting.'

It is possible that occasionally women turned the tables and used the excuse, consciously or not, of botanical drawing as a cover for travel and exploration. There are collections of drawings at Kew and the British Museum with tantalizing references; Mrs James Cookson's *Flowers Drawn and Painted after Nature in India*; Augusta Robley's *A selection of Madeira Flowers*; Arabella Roupell's *Specimens of the Flora of South Africa*; Mrs Julia Allport's Indian and Chinese flower paintings; Matilda Ayrton's drawings from Japan; Lady Maria Callcott in Brazil . . . there is a long list of such women but there are rarely more than a few brief and uninformative lines about their lives.

LEFT
Marianne North, who travelled with great energy and verve throughout the world, botanizing and painting.

RIGHT
White convolvulus and *Cestrum elegans*, one of many paintings Marianne North donated to Kew.

The best documented traveller is Marianne North. She was a dutiful Victorian daughter to her father, the M.P. Richard North, and had travelled to Syria and Egypt with him. When he died she decided to dedicate her life to his memory by painting flowers in remote lands. She painted in the U.S.A., Canada, Jamaica and Brazil in 1871–2; took a second trip to California, Japan, Borneo, Java and Ceylon in 1875–7; then to India in 1878–9. At the suggestion of Charles Darwin she went to Borneo, Australia, New Zealand and California in 1880. She travelled to South Africa in 1882–3; to the Seychelles in 1883–4; and to Chile in 1884–5. She not only left her paintings to Kew, she also commissioned and designed a building in which to house them. She was held in great respect by contemporaries for her indefatigable pursuit of botanical knowledge. Blunt, who denigrates the contribution of all early women artists, said her intrepid explorations did not make up for her lack of talent:

. . . her painting is almost wholly lacking in sensibility. The disagreeable impression made by her pictures is enhanced through her determination to display nearly eight hundred paintings in a gallery barely capable of showing fifty to advantage.

Botanical art was dependent on the means of reproduction, on the quality of the woodcuts, engravings, lithographs and colouring made from the original drawings. Sometimes the botanical artists were themselves the engravers and colourists; sometimes they relied on the skills of others. Joseph Banks, the first

Director of Kew, rich and well-travelled, had already employed Georg Ehret to paint the flowers from his Newfoundland expedition, and made experiments with engraving for the drawings brought back from his Australian voyage. At Kew he realized the importance of botanical drawing in establishing the scientific reputation of the gardens, and commissioned Franz and Ferdinand Bauer. Franz stayed at Kew as 'Botanick Painter to his Majesty', drawing and engraving, whilst his brother travelled extensively. They were the first Kew artists, and founders of an extraordinary tradition.

Another Kew artist who has recently been rediscovered is Margaret Meen. Little is known about her. She came from East Anglia, and at some point taught flower and insect painting. She exhibited at the Royal Academy from 1775–85. She became involved in a project to publish illustrations of exotic plants at Kew, but although the project was never finished, some of her illustrations remain. Wilfrid Blunt says of her 'she never quite rises above the level of a very highly gifted amateur'. However, Richard Mabey, who has recently re-evaluated her work, describes her as 'an artist of outstanding talent and vision'.

Also in the 1780s, William Curtis founded *Curtis' Botanical Magazine*. Curtis was an apothecary, associated with Philip Miller, the curator of the Chelsea Physic Garden, who spent ten years compiling *Flora Londinensis*, a record of plants growing within a 10-mile radius of London. This was a worthy effort but did not make money. Curtis decided on another strategy, a 'Botanical Magazine; or Flower Garden displayed' whose aim was to illustrate and describe

> . . . the most ornamental FOREIGN PLANTS, cultivated in the Open Ground, the Green-House and Stove . . . [with the illustrations] always drawn from the living plant, and coloured as near to nature as the imperfection of colouring will permit.

The magazine sold for one shilling and became a reference for botanists, artists and gardeners for more than a century.

In 1826 the editorship was taken over by William Hooker who drew as well as edited, although most of the engravings were undertaken by James Sowerby. Hooker became Professor of Botany at Glasgow University then, in 1841,

Director of Kew. The technique of lithography had been invented, and Hooker employed William Fitch to draw and engrave the paintings for the magazine, using the new technique. Fitch, who was originally a pattern drawer to a firm of calico printers, became the most important – and industrious – illustrator and engraver of his generation, and published nearly 10,000 drawings. His most well-known works were little wood-engravings, in a book, *Illustrations of the British Flora*, continuously in print until 1931. According to Stearn, 'it became a hobby of lady botanists in Britain to colour in these figures from living plants and accordingly to search for as many species as possible in a wild state.'

Joseph Hooker succeeded his father as Director of Kew in 1860, but he was an irritable and arrogant man, and treated Fitch increasingly badly. Fitch left Kew and the magazine in 1877, saying sadly, 'I feel heartsick, not only of the Bot. Mag. but even of Botany.'

Joseph Hooker's daughter, Harriet Anne, was married to Sir William Thistleton-Dyer, then Assistant Director at Kew (the man who was later to appoint the women gardeners in bloomers), and she helped out with some of the magazine plates, but Hooker had a 23-year-old second cousin called Mathilda Smith, who was known to be fond of drawing. He decided to teach her to draw botanically. She learnt quickly and drew skilfully, and within a year produced her first plate for the *Botanical Magazine*. She became an artist and lithographer for Hooker, illustrating his books of Kew plants. In 1898 she was officially appointed as artist to Kew Herbarium. As well as her work at Kew, she illustrated a work on New Zealand plants, another on the plants of Afghanistan, but from herbarium specimens. She did not travel herself but was praised for 're-animating dried, flattened specimens, often of an imperfect nature'. By her retirement from Kew in 1916, she had earned many honours: the Veitch Medal, election to the Linnaean Society, and being President of the Kew Guild. There were tributes to her skill, her 'beautiful and characteristic illustrations'. Wilfred Blunt, as usual, had reservations:

> Miss Smith . . . remained to the end a rather fumbling draughtsman, more remembered for her 'great pains' and 'untiring efforts' than for her skill, but esteemed for the charm of her personality.

Mathilda Smith,
botanical artist at
Kew and dutiful
cousin of Joseph
Hooker.

The *Botanical Magazine,* in its obituary note in 1926, also praised her
'devotion to duty' and her work for the church.

Whatever her feelings about her job, and the double-edged praise she
earned for her virtue at the expense of her art, Mathilda Smith had set a
precedent. Her famous successors at Kew have all been women. Lilian
Snelling was an artist and lithographer who first of all worked at the Edinburgh
Botanical Gardens, from 1916–21, and then became the official artist of the

Botanical Magazine (which had several changes of editorship and ownership) until 1952. She also illustrated a famous study of *The genus Paeonia* by F. C. Stern, and another on lilies. She received the coveted Victoria Medal of Honour from the R.H.S., and her citation praised her 'remarkable delicacy and accuracy of outlines, brilliancy of colour and intricate gradation of tone'.

Stella Ross-Craig began work at Kew in 1929, also when she was 23. She is regarded as one of the greatest of all Kew artists. She wrote an account for Wilfrid Blunt of how she draws:

> I first study the plant from all angles – as a sculptor might study a head when making a portrait – to grasp its *character*. To understand the structure of the flower it is sometimes necessary to use a magnifying glass. The most pleasing aspect having been decided upon, I sketch in the composition – lightly, but accurately as regards measurements. Leaves are adjusted, within scientific reason, to make an agreeable arrangement, and flowers that have been damaged . . . are replaced in the drawing by perfect specimens . . . The sketch completed, I work up the 'portrait' in detail, beginning with the fugitive parts such as quickly opening buds. Plants that change or wither rapidly present a very difficult problem to which there is only one answer – speed; and speed depends upon the immediate perception of the essential characteristics of the plant, a thorough knowledge of colours and colour mixing, and perfect co-ordination of hand and eye. Crocuses are especially awkward to manage when working indoors, for a bud one moment is an open flower the next, and it is necessary to move them at frequent intervals into a darker, or cooler, place.

Her most outstanding work is a scholarly 31-volume edition of native British plants (a source book for, amongst others, Miriam Rothschild). Every native plant is drawn in extraordinary detail, its root formation, reproductive organs, the texture of its leaf, and its flower, fruit, berry or seed, as well as the overall shape and form of the plant.

Mary Grierson is another well-known Kew artist. She trained originally in domestic science and worked as a cook in Harley Street, London. During the Second World War, she took a job making maps from aerial photographs. A fellow worker was a wild flower fanatic, and persuaded her to begin drawing.

Sorbus Esserteauiana

She then started to paint illustrations for her firm's business reports, and the firm recompensed her by paying for her to attend a course on botanical illustration given by artist John Nash, which included frequent visits to Cedric Morris's garden. (Cedric Morris was an artist and a mentor for Constance Spry and Beth Chatto.) In 1960, almost by accident, she applied for a job at Kew as Exhibitions Officer, but her portfolio was so good that the interviewer appointed her instead as Botanical Artist. She painted herbarium specimens, like her predecessors, but also undertook visits to Hawaii and Israel. She has exhibited as an artist; produced a series on flowers of the hedgerow; designed

ABOVE
Iris iberica by Mary
Grierson.

LEFT
Sorbus esserteauiana by Lilian Snelling.

ABOVE
Ochagaria cornea by Stella Ross-Craig.

postage stamps, and commemorative plates; and has been commissioned to paint a model of an eighteenth-century harpsichord.

Paradoxically, as women's contributions to botanical art were becoming recognized, the new technique of photography began to replace drawing and painting; and from being central to writing and thinking about the properties of plants and gardens, botanical art has become peripheral to them. Gertrude Jekyll and Ellen Willmott were enthusiastic photographers, exercising a control over the medium that would have been impossible with drawing, engraving or printing. Colour printing has improved dramatically over the last

20 years, and few gardening books – including this – are now without their quota of glossy photographs. But whilst photographs may give a relatively easily obtained impression of a garden and its plants, the display and synthesis of detail in a drawing of a plant is still unmatchable.

Ruskin, who hated botanists and who thought it prurient to pry into the 'obscene processes' of plant reproduction, nevertheless argued that drawing flowers was a way of seeing and understanding their beauty. 'It is difficult to give the accuracy of attention necessary to see their beauty without drawing them.' For him, drawing was an active process of perceiving, creation as well as documentation. There was an acute difference between

> . . . attentive drawing which gives the cadence and relation of masses in a group, and the mere copying of each flower in an unconsidered huddle.

Photography is an accurate – even if contrived and staged – picture of what exists; light intensity, colour balance, forms and groupings are reflected in the eye of the camera. Painting introduces another dimension, an idealization, a vision, a perfect and unspoilt version, a transformation and distillation. Photographers such as Valerie Finnis have used the medium of photography in this way, to produce a kind of photographic bouquet, but, as she herself admits, it does not compare with the intricacies and intensity of painting.

Even although the genre of botanical art is now a minor one, there are many contemporary artists who continue to share this preoccupation with 'seeing'. Any list is a somewhat arbitrary recital of talents but those who continue the remarkable Kew tradition and illustrate for the *Kew Magazine* include Marjorie Blamey, whose past life included a spell as a dairy farmer; Jill Coombs, trained as a ceramicist, who has also illustrated a book for Beth Chatto; Christabel King, a botanist; Rodella Purves who also works for the Edinburgh Botanical Garden; Pandora Sellars, previously a textile designer; and Margaret Stones who was a nurse, and learned to paint during a long spell in hospital as a patient. As is frequently the case for women, their routes to their profession have mostly been circuitous.

The story of two well-known contemporary flower painters illustrates, as with gardening, how it is possible to earn distinction after many years of distraction. Lys de Bray is a flower painter, whose published work includes

Fantastic Garlands, an anthology of flowers and plants from Shakespeare; and *Cottage Garden Year*, an illustrated diary of her own cottage garden. Now in her sixties, she has had a varied and unsettled career, as a medical secretary, a quality control planner, and as a housewife. She has always gardened, 'violently'. She burnt down three sheds, and used a pickaxe on the concrete flooring in order to create her first garden in a backyard in Bournemouth. This included a tiny pond, a tiny lawn, a cherry tree, a hydrangea under a leaking gutter, and a 'Peace' rose. Her second garden was a walled cottage garden in a small town. She became interested in 'strange plants' – she planted flowers because of their names, unsure at first of what they would look like. Her garden eventually became very well known, and much visited. Recently, she has moved to the countryside, where she is creating her third garden out of a bare field. Its centrepiece, and her starting point for designing it, is a large Victorian urn she was given as a present.

Lys de Bray began drawing only in 1972, when she was recuperating after a spell in hospital. A friend brought her a sheaf of wild flowers: elderflower, sorrel, campion and bluebells. She took the flowers home and tried to draw them. At first she tried pastels but they were not accurate enough so she borrowed some drawing pens. She felt obsessed by them, and went to bed at dusk in order to catch the dawn light to finish drawing. It took four days of constant concentration. She discovered she could draw, and began to produce line drawings and prints. She went out cold-selling in her sports car, and managed to find customers. 'I did sell them, they were well printed and methodical.' Her first efforts were line drawings but then she gradually attempted colour. Her first contract was with the publisher Weidenfeld & Nicolson, for a book on wild flowers. Although she basically wanted to paint flowers from her garden, she has had to supplement her income – as Redouté also did – with what she calls 'kitsch': china plates and cups, cards and notepaper.

Her garden and her painting are separate activities, and she has 'powerful relationships' with each of them; they have their own impetus but they are also interdependent. Her garden is her library: 'I grow things that I might paint for their fascination or beauty.'

Drawing and painting for Lys de Bray means accuracy, noting with precision all the minute variations of form and colour in a single flower or leaf;

RIGHT
A photograph of a flower bouquet by Valerie Finnis. It contains 103 different kinds of flower, arranged in a copy of a seventeenth-century tulip-holder.

BELOW
This photograph by Valerie Finnis of autumnal shrubs and trees in David Scott's garden catches an effect that would be hard to reproduce as a botanical painting.

Paphiopedilum insigne
painted by Lys de
Bray.

but unless there is also vitality, a catching and transposing of the living plant, it is empty copy. 'You can tell when a painting has been lovingly done.'

In the garden she is making, she wants plants that are lusty, not 'miffy'; plants that do not need 'nursemaiding'. She refers to all her plants as 'he' – as a revolt against the general tendency to call everything 'she' – and sometimes addresses them directly as people. 'I'll just tuck him in here . . . he needs watering . . . this should suit you, my dear.' Her front garden contains beds of modern roses, which she loves to paint, especially the coffee and terracotta shades. She has no time for feminist analysis but nevertheless thinks that there is a typically British gardening woman, 'middle-aged, eccentric and exceedingly positive'. Strong women, she believes, should not be afraid to apologize for their mistakes, especially if they need to earn the respect of men whom they employ. She has had some help in laying out her field. 'You have to delegate the boring bits, and realize you no longer have the muscle.' She believes that, like all committed gardeners, she is inspired by 'divine discontent'.

The second of these two painters is Margaret Mee. She has the forcefulness of imagery, the power and éclat and individuality of some of the greatest illustrators. She has followed in the traditions of the plant hunters but, whereas for them acquisition and transportation of exceedingly rare plants from remote corners of the Earth and their introduction into Britain have been a crowning achievement, she has been concerned above all with conservation and describing and maintaining plants in their natural habitats.

Margaret Mee was born in 1909, and trained at the Camberwell School of Art with the artist Victor Pasmore. Amongst her other activities, she was an active and militant trade unionist in the 1930s. In 1952 she and her husband went to Brazil, where he was a commercial artist, and she taught drawing.

At the age of 47, with a woman colleague, she decided to take a holiday hiking and painting in the Amazon region. They did not have much money or time but for Margaret Mee it was the beginning of an obsession. She went back to the Amazon and its tributaries, particularly the river Negro, whenever she could raise the money and find the time. She painted in gouache and, however oblivious she was to conventional explorers' supplies, her paper and paints were meticulously protected, and her first care in an emergency. Her hazardous journeys were usually under-resourced. She often travelled by herself; she depended on local transport, and frequently had problems with food supplies. As well as starving, she was bitten, stung and nearly drowned, and sometimes physically attacked by white settlers. Despite these dangers, she resolutely collected and drew plants, painting them in their natural habitats. She identified several new species of bromeliads and orchids.

Margaret Mee kept a diary of her journeys, which was later published. She cared passionately about the destruction of the rainforests, the senseless clearing of vegetation, the slaughter of birds and animals, and, above all, about the plight of local Indian tribes. She was extremely gentle and self-effacing, and although she was obliged to carry a revolver (which she once used to save her life) she hated all killing.

She became famous in Brazil, and was a friend of the extraordinary Brazilian landscape gardener Burlo Marx, to whom she gave many of the plants she collected, and was honoured by the Brazilian government. She returned to Britain occasionally for exhibitions, to see friends, and for medical treatment, including a hip replacement which enabled her to go back into the jungle on more physically demanding expeditions. She was killed tragically,

ABOVE AND LEFT
Margaret Mee
painting the Amazon
moonflower in situ.

not in the jungle, but in a road accident in Leicestershire, at the age of 79.

Her paintings are stunning and instantly recognizable, not merely because of their exotic subject matter but for their boldness and richness, and the way in which the plants are seen as part of their natural habitat. Her most famous painting, completed just before her death, is of the Amazon moonflower, a night-flowering cactus. It flowers infrequently, and its flowering time is extremely short, less than one night. Margaret Mee saw the plant once in flower in 1964 but was unable to paint it then. She found it on three more occasions, but it was not in flower. Finally, on her last expedition, 24 years later, she located it by the river Negro and, after an all-night vigil, painted it by torchlight.

Drawing and painting flowers was once the other side of the coin to growing them. We think of it now as a minor art, a reflection of a more leisurely age. This may have been the case for some women living in enforced idleness, but it was also a major enterprise, part of the great botanical adventure. Even for those whose drawing skills are limited, it is still a way of seeing.

CHAPTER EIGHT

PLANTS FOR SALE

The history of gardens is also the history of plants. The nurserymen who have selected, grown, sold and distributed the plants have played a key role in determining how gardens have looked. English gardening has always made use of an extraordinarily wide range of plants. Russell Page, the garden designer, suggests this is partly temperamental, a constitutional liking for 'a state of flux . . . a native dislike for a coldly logical formulation or the termination of a spoken phrase . . . a slow process of wooing growing things into giving their best'. But it is also climatic. The lack of extremes of temperature means that thousands of plants can be tried out; the swing of the seasons and the inconstant weather means that growing plants is always a gamble. The hunt for rare or unusual plants, and then the struggle to keep them, is an English gardening obsession.

The most scholarly historian of nurseries is the antiquarian, John Harvey. He has examined bills of sale, wills, catalogues, bankruptcy notices, all manner of deeds, tickets and dockets, to trace the histories of the early nurseries.

The first nurseries depended on a number of factors besides skill in cultivating plants: on their nearness to cities or prospective purchasers; on the availability of transport; on the development of world trade and colonialism

Beth Chatto's water garden. She has created a number of different habitats in her garden; here the plants relish the damp conditions.

for the introduction of new plants; and on the aesthetics of contemporary garden design and fashion. In his book *Early Nurserymen* Harvey described the typical nurseryman:

> Learning their trade by family training or by apprenticeship to a gardener, possibly the chief gardener to a great estate, they would go on to become assistants to such estate gardeners or foremen in nurseries. In the course of time, and if their luck held or their savings were sufficient, they would found a nursery of their own, or occasionally buy a partnership in one . . . Not infrequently they married the daughter or sister of another gardener, nurseryman or botanist.

Shreds of evidence of women's influence in the past have filtered down to us. Women were wives and assistants to nurserymen, and sometimes inheritors of the nursery. Next door to John Gerard in Holborn, London, in the seventeenth century, Mistress Tuggy continued to breed her much admired 'gillyflowers' or carnations after her husband Ralph Tuggy died. In 1726, James Pullen, a Bristol nurseryman, left his eldest daughter Sarah Pullen '. . . all my Fruit Trees, Greene Trees, Flowering Trees and Trees and Flowers in the Home Garden'.

The Brompton Park nursery, which supplied the Duchess of Portland throughout the latter part of the eighteenth century, is described as belonging to the firm of 'Mary, William and Joseph Kirke', although no one knows what Mary did, apart from – presumably – supply some of the capital.

Often nursery catalogues were illustrated by the wives or daughters of the nurserymen. John Loudon, nineteenth-century garden designer and writer, comments on the catalogue of Brentford nursery 'beautifully illustrated by drawings from nature' by Elizabeth Ronalds, the daughter of the nurseryman. Loudon mentions other Victorian nurserywomen in his *Encyclopedia of Gardening*: Elizabeth Wheeler, 'nursery and seedswoman' in Gloucester; Ann Ford, specializing in trees, in Exeter; Mary Rogers in Knutsford, selling flowering shrubs; Catherine Mullock in Nantwich 'nurseryman and seedsman'.

Women assisted and very occasionally took over in the nurseries. Unlisted and unacknowledged, they were often the backbone of the enterprise but, as

Harvey carefully documents, running a nursery was a skilled and demanding business, then as now.

> The basis of nurseries is plantsmanship: the ability to get seeds to germinate, plants to grow and above all to flower and fruit, and not simply to do so but to display the fullest perfection of which the species is capable.

This process may take years of patient watching for a particular species. Plantsmanship is not the whole story; business and marketing skills also count. The successful nursery owner is:

> . . . running a business which is to provide him . . . with at least a livelihood. Every plant or batch of plants has to be labelled, if possible with the currently accepted scientific name . . . [each plant] is [also] a business asset which needs to be registered in and out of stock books . . . and described in bills sent to individual customers. Complaints from those customers, requests for information and for plants not in stock; negotiations with landlords or agents over the land for the nursery or for expansion; the preparation of catalogues and the exhibits for . . . shows; travel, commercial or scientific . . . [the] attending of meetings and conferences: all these have to be fitted in.

Plants and business: how do these square up? For many women who grow and sell plants, the emphasis has been on the plants rather than the business. Often the women have some other source of income and the propagation of plants is not so much income generating as an overflow from other gardening activities, an extension of the obsession to nurse plants to life. Margery Fish, who in her day was as well known in gardening circles as Vita Sackville-West, is the classic example of this absorption in the whole process of gardening.

Margery Fish was a secretary and personal assistant to the editor of the *Daily Mail* for most of her professional working life and showed no interest in gardening. Then in her late forties she married Walter Fish, the editor of the *Mail*, and they bought a house in Somerset, called East Lambrook Manor. Both the house and garden were in a bad state, and they set about restoration. Walter had very definite ideas about what to do and expected them to be carried out. With enviable equanimity Margery Fish describes how they worked together, in her book, *We Made a Garden*.

LEFT
Margery Fish
framed in the door
of the Malthouse of
East Lambrook
Manor. She
propagated her
plants on the
windowsill.

BELOW
The path leading
from the back of
the house. The
planting looks
casual and cottagey,
but it needs
vigilance to
maintain the
balance between the
many self-seeding
plants.

RIGHT
Polygonatum
flourishing in a
shady corner.

I learnt a great deal from Walter in that first year of gardening. The first thing I learnt was that he knew a great deal more about the subject than I thought he did.

Walter argued that the garden needed form and structure, and that the heavy clay soil needed plenty of nutrients, but he was essentially a fairweather gardener, a 'dahlia, delphinium and lupin man'. He disliked many of the plants Margery acquired. Plants he did not like or thought unhealthy he would simply pull up, leaving them on the path 'like a row of dead rats'. He had no hesitation about walking on her plants if they were in the way. 'He never worried about my plants or smothering them with great piles of earth.' To decorate the walls he bought a gross of stuffed animals from a London saleroom, and mounted them everywhere. 'Heads, antlers and horns sprouted from every available wall, inside and out. Walter used to chuckle about the heads . . .' Walter Fish's obsession was dahlias. He made no distinctions as to colour, and they were extremely flashy. They were planted and lifted on Stock Exchange holidays, 1 May and 1 November, and required ceremonial and ritual labour.

I was permitted to get barrowloads of manure and cans of water but he would not trust me to do more. In after years when he could not do the heavy jobs I had to plant them but he always stood by to see I didn't cheat.

Although Margery Fish was devastated by the loss, fortunately for gardening history Walter died, and she was able to pursue her own very different ideas about gardening. She rejected wholeheartedly the formality of the Edwardian gardens of her youth. She was influenced by cottage gardens, the idea of informality, native plants such as geraniums, hellebores and primroses growing in exuberant profusion and being allowed to seed themselves. The paths became tapestries of small creeping plants. She called it 'jungle gardening' but, despite the profusion, she maintained the garden to an extremely high standard, and knew the whereabouts of all her plants, keeping watch for special seedlings, clearing small spaces for the most vulnerable plants, or growing them in troughs and stone sinks. It looked like low-maintenance gardening but, in reality, required a very high level of maintenance and alertness to keep the delicate balance between so many competing plants.

Margery Fish collected plants avidly. Like many others, she was influenced by Nancy Lindsay – the disintegrating zinc bucket came out for her too. She and Phyllis Reiss from nearby Tintinhull in Somerset were taken on plant-hunting expeditions in a chauffeur-driven car by another near neighbour, Mrs Clive from Brympton d'Evercy. The chauffeur was instructed to stop the car at small cottages where the gardens might harbour a long-lost plant. She was a friend of 'Aunt May' Amory (a cousin of the Amorys at Knightshayes in Devon) who gave her many plants. She became obsessed with unusual forms of plants, doubles, and variegations. In later years, although generous with her plants, she was cagey about where she had obtained them. She always carried a spade and a sack in her car and, if she spotted good leaf-mould, would stop instantly, whatever she was wearing and wherever she was going, in order to shovel it up.

Margery Fish wrote several books and gave broadcasts on the radio. Her direct and lively style was popular, and her knowledge about cottage gardening and native plants was unrivalled. She was invited to lecture; her talks were mesmerizing. She would illustrate them by holding up bits of the plants she had grown, and then sell the cuttings or plants she had propagated, which she carried around with her, also in the boot of her car. She was not materialistic but relished making money from her books and from her plants. She grew trays of cuttings and germinated seeds on the window ledges of her large barn, the Malthouse. These would be potted on and sold in her nursery. Several part-time staff were employed to help in the nursery, which thrived as her reputation grew. Groups and tours booked to see her garden, and then bought plants at the nursery. Penelope Hobhouse was one of her customers, and described the pleasure of buying from someone so willing to discuss plants.

She worked at a formidable pace, writing first thing in the morning and after dusk until the small hours, and gardening the rest of the time. She kept up this brisk pace almost until her death in 1969. Inevitably after this the garden lapsed but it is now being restored and is open to the public. The nursery is still there, rather more organized, with glasshouses, tunnels and stock-beds; and houses the national collection of geraniums.

Many nurseries grew like this out of an obsession with plants. Beth Chatto is one of the best-known contemporary nurserywomen, through her writings

ABOVE
Beth Chatto tending her herbaceous plants.

ABOVE RIGHT
Semi-hardy plants in pots on her sheltered terrace.

and her garden, as well as through her extremely efficiently-run nursery. She has written at length about how she became a gardener. As a young woman she knew the late Sir Cedric Morris, part of the charmed Essex circle of painters and gardeners which included John Nash, Mary Grierson and Constance Spry. Her husband, a fruit farmer, also studied the ecology of garden plants and gave her the idea of selecting plants suited to the environment. Before marriage she trained as a teacher then, whilst staying at home with two small children and fighting bouts of depression, she was befriended by her neighbour Mrs Desmond Underwood, the 'Silver Queen' (specializing in grey and silver-leaved plants), from Ramparts Nursery in Colchester (a local politician, holder of a Victoria Medal of Honour, and a formidable woman). Mrs Underwood levered her out of domesticity and persuaded her to help found a flower-arranging club in Colchester. In creating arrangements, Beth Chatto used the unusual flowers, leaves and seedheads she grew in her garden or found growing in wild places. She found the gardening therapeutic.

> The garden has for many people become far more than an attractive addition to the home. It is a form of therapy. The dedication and devotion needed, and the response from plants, provides both solace and inspiration, supportive through many crises that inevitably come in the course of life.

Beth Chatto opened her nursery for unusual plants in 1967 after her husband retired from fruit growing. The nursery was on land unsuitable for farming:

. . . a few acres of wasteland in a hollow between two farms . . . dry stony gravel on the upper south-facing slope, saturated black silt over clay in the hollow, with a spring-fed ditch running through the lowest level.

They built a house on the dry gravelly slope and set out to make a garden around it, which could display the plants they had selected. She wrote about making it in two books, each focusing on a different site in the garden: *The Dry Garden* and *The Damp Garden*. *Plant Portraits* is a collection of descriptions of some of her favourite plants and their growing habits (illustrated by Jill Coombs, the botanical artist mentioned in the last chapter).

The nursery also exhibited at Chelsea Flower Show, winning a series of gold medals, and the Victoria Medal of Honour for Beth Chatto. She has described in her *Garden Notebook* the passionate involvement in showing at Chelsea, the perfect timing and last-minute manoeuvres that any successful exhibitor must master, whatever the quality of the plants. Pushing through the dense crowds by the garish and overwhelming displays in the main show tent, visitors would find her stand, displayed as a miniature garden, was always a haven, with subtle contrasts and delicate-looking plants in exquisite arrangements.

Her nursery built up slowly, and then began to sell by mail order. Its reputation grew, alongside Beth Chatto's other activities. It now employs a permanent staff of six men and eleven women, with additional labour in summer, and uses computerized stock lists. Apart from having a love of plants and skill in raising them, Beth Chatto is an astute businesswoman, keen to use the most appropriate technology, keeping careful notes on planting schedules, making sure the nursery is immaculately laid out so it is easy to find plants, managing her loyal staff with kindness and competence, training students – each task undertaken with assurance and efficiency.

Small and spare, she is blessed with energy and vitality. Few of her staff can match her pace as she sets off round the garden or nursery. On the coldest February day in that bleak Essex landscape, with freezing north-easterly winds, she may still be found planting outside. She also finds time to maintain a small vegetable garden, where she grows little-known salad vegetables, such as rocket and lambs' lettuce, recommended to her long ago by Cedric Morris. She makes her own bread and loves cooking. She still displays talent for flower arrangements, with jugs and vases of flowers from the garden or beautifully dried flowers in winter.

She is a no-nonsense gardener; tasks are undertaken promptly whenever they need doing. In her garden notebook she described an incident when she was watering her plants. A small boy whose mother was visiting the nursery asked her:

> 'Does Mrs Chatto work here?'
> 'Yes, I am Mrs Chatto.'
> 'But you're working. Aren't you famous then? I thought you wrote books.'
> 'Well, sometimes people tell me I am famous, but I am still myself, and whether I am famous or not we must rescue these plants, so please help me and see the hose doesn't tangle with the pots.'

The conversation is typical; so is her memory of it, careful enough to write it afterwards in her diary, with a slightly wry comment.

> I must be a disappointment to those romantics who expect to find a graceful figure deadheading the roses, but occasionally it is I who am disconcerted, as when I saw starry-eyed illusion drain from one small boy's eyes.

Through understanding the needs and origins of plants and placing them in harmonious combinations in often problematic areas, Beth Chatto, like Margery Fish, has made her mark on our gardens.

Others less well known have also had an effect. Elizabeth Strangman at Washfield Nursery, near Sissinghurst in Kent, has the sort of collection of rare plants that makes avid gardeners tongue-tied. The plants are immaculately looked after in the ancient cold-frames she inherited from Hilda Davenport-Jones – one of the earliest women to achieve a degree from Reading University, and a friend of the Amorys at Knightshayes, Vita Sackville-West, and others in the plant networks. Elizabeth Strangman trained at Studley College and, after a short spell working for Constance Spry, was for many years Miss Davenport-Jones's assistant. Her nursery is small and she manages it with just one helper. Her reputation for looking after difficult plants is unsurpassed; newly collected plants, such as some of the corydalis and epimediums from

China, are given to her to propagate. She spends years working on certain strains of plants such as hellebores, hand-pollinating and breeding them. She no longer supplies plants by mail order and sells retail only. Her nursery is rather like a gourmet restaurant, where the chef has spent a long time perfecting a dish which no one else has even tried. She describes it as 'bloodymindedness' to grow the plants she is interested in, rather than follow market trends.

One of the newer nurseries which combines business acumen with stunning plantsmanship is Blackthorn, in Hampshire. Their spring stand at the R.H.S. show at Vincent Square, London, is showstopping; the plants, mainly hellebores early in the year, looking as if they were fresh from Redouté. The nursery is run by Sue and Robin White, and is a modern success story: Blackthorn was created from nothing in seven years.

Sue White in her newly created woodland garden, taking a rare break from the nursery.

They had no capital, and not much experience, only a determination to grow plants. Her husband had horticultural training, she did not. They took a lease on a derelict walled garden, first of all growing vegetable crops following college notes, then turning to herbs, pot plants, or anything which would make money – even holly wreaths at Christmas, one of the most painful of all florists' jobs. They were wholesalers, supplying whatever market they could. Later, they saved enough to buy a bare field and, because they could afford nothing else, lived in a mobile home for two years whilst they developed the nursery.

From there they went from strength to strength. Her husband had lived, breathed and dreamed of plants all his life, and Sue White became sucked into the dream too. Their work was also their hobby. They decided a wholesale nursery was too soul-destroying: taking hundreds of thousands of cuttings and rearing them like battery-fed hens. They cared about the quality of individual plants; they acquired an increasing number of tunnels; mist-propagated by hand since different plants had differing needs; mixed all their own composts; worked out their own plant feeds; and potted on new stock plants every year. They experimented with new plants. She took on alpines, and tried some breeding experiments with them. They worked from dawn to dusk, and into the night, and tried not to worry about keeping detailed plant records.

They decided they would go for quick turnover, since they wanted their plants to be sold in tip-top condition, but the care of the plants was too demanding to spare much time for sales. They did not want to take on extra staff: 'The more staff we employ, the less we have contact with the plants, the poorer the standard.' They took the high-risk strategy of opening only two days a week, Fridays and Saturdays from March to October, firmly turned down all visitors at any other time, and refused to sell by mail order. They employ part-time staff on sales days and for help with propagating, and have one full-time assistant, Pam, who was trained at Merrist Wood College. As they are now well known they are sent cuttings and seeds; they are on the exchange circuit. Customers have flooded in, despite the restricted hours – little wonder since the Whites pride themselves above all on the quality and range of their plants.

It gives me a tremendous boost when customers like our plants, real pleasure when they come back and say we haven't lost anything this year.

The relentless pace has reached its climax. As the Whites have earned money they have been able to have a house built and begun to create their own garden. They have even taken a holiday. 'What is the point if we don't?' They try to have a day off a week, although they do not often succeed; more often Sue White spends her rare spare time in shopping or even a walk with the dog, just for a break. It has been a life of total partnership, total immersion, but the strategy is paying off: 'We've done all the donkey work – but we're reaping the benefits now.'

Nicky's Rock Garden Nursery is a partnership of a more relaxed and convivial kind; the balance is on the side of the plants and the business is a bonus – it pays for the hobby. Bob and Diana Darle live in a small semi-detached house near Honiton in Devon. She was a shorthand typist, he is a carpenter who repairs antique furniture. They used to keep birds as pets for their three daughters, until the bird-feed became too expensive, then they turned to alpines, almost by accident. Eleven years ago they went to Axminster market and bought six alpine plants without even knowing their names. They were hooked. They bought a Collins *Guide to Alpines*, identified their six plants which included *Aethionema* × 'Warley Rose' and *Veronica prostrata*, and bought a carload more from an alpine nursery. Bob became interested in propagation and rigged up a small glasshouse. Diana did the rest, which included keeping a meticulous card index file on every single plant they have ever grown. 'I like lists, I'm a list person.' They sent away for seeds from the various alpine societies, to America, to individual collectors.

The nursery was named in honour of their youngest daughter, Nicky, to try to interest her in plants. They started it because they had plants to spare, and wanted to cover their costs, although their plants are sold so cheaply that each one, however rare, feels like a present. They make very little money, 'anything that's labour intensive never does'. Each plant is grown in the garden first, and then, if it is successful, it is propagated and potted up. The walls, crevices and paths in their little garden overflow with plants.

They have a stock of between 800–1000 alpines, and make a point of trying out 200 new species each year. As their stock grows so does their library; they scour second-hand bookshops for books about alpines. They stress it is a hobby. They describe books and alpines as their 'two vices'. They twinkle with pleasure and good humour. They love talking about alpines, and welcome casual visitors to their garden and nursery at whatever time of day. They attend Alpine Society meetings and south of England shows, sometimes exhibiting and selling. Diana has abandoned almost all attempts at housework in their small cottage, 'Thank goodness', and they live in happy chaos, spending every possible moment amongst their alpines. They chide each other gently, finish each other's sentences. 'We're a pretty good team.'

Carol Klein is another Devon nurserywoman, who some see as the inheritor of the mantle of Margery Fish. At her small nursery, Glebe Cottage Plants, she grows delicate, subtle plants, which she exhibits at various shows in clever and glowing combinations, winning gold medal after gold medal. However, her background could not have been more different from Margery Fish. It is doubtful whether Carol has ever ridden in a chauffeur-driven car or, for that matter, a taxi. She and her plants are transported in battered vans, usually hired, and with a propensity to breaking down in awkward places. In public she wears punk clothes; at home, in summer, she gardens in skimpy dresses and army boots, which she wears sockless and without laces.

Carol Klein used to teach art in boys' schools in inner London. She would take small groups of boys off to Kew – when it was a penny to get in – to sketch and take photographs. She and the boys loved it; some are still in touch with her. She moved to Devon 14 years ago when she had had enough of London and wanted more space. She taught for several years in Devon then finally gave it up, apart from bouts of supply teaching when in need of money.

She had always loved plants but had been confined to a first-floor window box in London, in which she grew flowers that trailed right down the front of the house, and caused dissent with her neighbours. Glebe Cottage was very isolated, and semi-derelict. It was a small stone house standing at the top of a very sharp slope. The acre of land around the house had been used mainly for car-breaking, with a sideline in chickens and rabbits housed in filthy sheds. Carol and her partner Neil had to shift 15 tons of old metal and assorted rubbish to clear the ground. 'I did most of the heavy stuff. We hired a mechanical digger for one day.'

They had little money to spare, and no connections or gardening links. Whilst Neil concentrated on renovating the house, Carol was determined to

Carol Klein explaining her catalogue to a visitor at the Chelsea Flower Show. Her explanations reflect her exuberant enthusiasm for the colour and form of plants.

make a garden. The only plants already there were honeysuckle and violets. She bought a very small greenhouse so that she could grow cuttings and seeds; and blew her precious savings of £200 on trees and shrubs. She searched junk yards for consignments of stone for paving, and painstakingly terraced the slope and made paths and steps. She grew vegetables, 'I had to feed us.' By then she had two daughters, both summer babies. She remembers 'looking out the window, feeding them, seeing dandelions and the finches on the thistles and thinking, "Oh well".'

She describes herself and her partner as 'doting parents', although as the garden became increasingly more important Neil took over more of the house-work and childcare. 'He does everything although he doesn't always do it well . . . !'

She started selling plants at the local market, where she met an older woman called Sonia Roffey. She was a flower arranger and a wonderful gardener;

Carol always half-hoped that customers would not come so she could spend more time talking about plants and gardens with Sonia. When the customers did come she was fascinated by how Sonia dealt with them, the way she gave them confidence to experiment with plants.

> I've never heard anyone else put across so well what a plant is and does, what kind of personality it has. She talked to people to sell them a plant and she told them all about it, absolutely everything.

Sadly Sonia died of cancer, but her memory continues to be an inspiration.

Carol Klein took on an evening class in cottage gardening, which she ran for four years. She enjoyed the experience, 'We had such a good time, people were glowing you know.' She also exhibited her plants locally and decided to have a go at the R.H.S. shows.

> I got on a coach and went to the R.H.S. Great Autumn show. I was impressed by the Ramparts Nursery display of silver-leaved plants. I went round and talked, I looked under the skirts of the stands, I asked questions, I wondered if I could do it.

Marina Christopher, a partner in Green Farm nursery, modestly organizing her rows of unusual plants.

The shows provide an opportunity to become known, to keep in touch and swap with other nurseries, and to sell plants. This has been a successful strategy for Carol Klein and she, in turn, is part of a gardening network; but because of the remoteness of her nursery, she also started to sell by mail order. 'I hate it. It's frantic. I'm hopeless at book-keeping, absolutely useless.'

She describes herself as totally obsessional.

The only way to start from scratch is just to shut everything else out and concentrate on the plants, if you've got enough energy.

In the end, it is the plants which count; and how they enhance one another.

It's a generalization, but men's gardens seem to be collections of plants for the sake of them, whereas most women's gardens are *plantings*, plants that grow with one another.

In the sunshine, Carol Klein's house is covered with flowering wisteria and other creepers, so that the front door is hidden and unusable. The garden, sloping downhill, is full of bees and wonderful scents, waves of blossom and colour, artlessly arranged, and it is difficult to believe that not long ago there was little growing there at all.

Marina Christopher is another of the new generation of nurserywomen. A small neat woman, dressed in jeans and T-shirt, she has a Ph.D. in botany and marine biology, and at one time thought of an academic career. In the end she came to feel that academic botany was a 'narrow-minded' subject; botanical training was about 'the inside of plants not the outside'. The difficulty of finding employment after university led her to take a temporary job in an orchard and she realized her leanings were more pragmatic, and more practical: she became interested in growing things. After a short-term job surveying the flora of the Oxford canal, she decided to take on part-time gardening work. By chance, she ended up gardening for Miss Christie-Miller, the alpine specialist who had also helped Valerie Finnis; and selling and propagating for Elizabeth Parker Jervis at Marten's Hall Farm, who ran a small and very specialized nursery, and who had been another protégée of the plantsman E. A. Bowles. This was a useful apprenticeship and she then tried to set up her own nursery, selling native plants which were pollinated by insects, a particular interest of hers. Getting started proved almost impossible as it was difficult to raise capital and she had no proper facilities, no ground, only a rented cottage, and too little time left over from her other jobs. The conservation movement was not yet popular and, when she did sell plants at markets, she would hear comments like, 'I can grow weeds like that in my own garden'.

She is now a partner in another nursery, Green Farm. This specializes in semi-tender plants and shrubs, and is closely associated with the much-visited garden Jenkyn Place in Hampshire; the other partner John Coke is a son of its owners. The nursery is well-connected in every sense; Marina has brought to it a practical and down-to-earth approach, complementing the plantsmanship, extending the range of plants, making time for customers and, in common with all those running nurseries, working gruelling hours throughout spring and summer, yet somehow fitting in private and domestic life around the insatiable needs of the plants.

These women are a small sample of a thriving trade. There are many dozens of little nurseries throughout the country, part business, part hobby, part garden overflow, part collector's passion, women with 'an eye for a plant'. The routes to these achievements have been various; Maureen Iddon in Southport, a grandmother who like Beth Chatto was a flower arranger, and whose tiny nursery is shared by her son, now a well-known flower arranger on the northern circuit; Pat Perry, north of Scarborough, a journalist on the local paper until she discovered a chance seedling of osteospermum, registered it and obtained plant breeder's rights, and made a small fortune enabling her to set up her own nursery full-time alongside her husband's tearoom; Joan Fussey, in the North Yorkshire moors, whose remote smallholding has been turned into a home for a few plant treasures; or Anita Thorp in Leicestershire, another alpinist, whose plants are stacked in their hundreds in the narrow back garden of her bungalow. It is impossible to do justice to the effort and talent of so many women. The garden centres and wholesale nurseries are commercially run, and profit-orientated, and offer familiar plants at more or less reasonable prices. But the cutting edge is elsewhere; it is these small enterprises and obsessions which bring vitality to the gardening world.

CHAPTER NINE

FLOWERS AND FRIENDSHIP

T he earliest gardening associations, dating back to the sixteenth century, were the florists' societies. These were clubs devoted to the breeding and growing of certain varieties of plants: anemones, tulips, auriculas, polyanthus, carnations and pinks, hyacinth and ranunculus until the 1800s; and then expanded to include the 'new flowers' – dahlias, pansies and chrysanthemums. The florists' societies were originally centred around Norwich in Norfolk where Huguenot weavers had settled. Later on, florists' societies became widespread; pinks in Paisley; pansies in Derbyshire; polyanthus in Sheffield.

The societies were gardening clubs for raising, showing and discussing plants. Their meetings were frequent – often weekly – and convivial, held in local inns and taverns. A frequent toast of the Paisley Florist Society was to 'Flowers and Friendship'. Ruth Duthie, in her book on florists' societies, *Florist's Flowers and Societies*, includes this account of a Florists' Feast of 1770.

On Tuesday last a great Feast of Gardiners call'd Florists was held in the Dog in Richmond Hill, at which were present about 130 in Number; after Dinner several shew'd their Flowers and five ancient and judicious Gardiners were Judges to determine whose Flowers excelled.

Church Hill Cottage in Kent,
one of the gardens encouraged to open under the National Garden Scheme.

These feasts sometimes had a pagan theme. The goddess Flora, in the form of a small statuette, stood at the head of the table and a toast was drunk to her. The Paisley Florist Society recorded their difficulties in 1804 after their statuette of Flora was accidentally dropped and her head was broken.

> . . . inquiries [were] directed to a celebrated head shop . . . in which a variety of colossal and Lilliputian heads were exhibited and they found that none of these heads would fit except the head of Mary Queen of Scots by a little alteration might suit, but as the price demanded was two Guineas, they thought proper to decline the purchase – poor Flora may perhaps remain sometime longer without a head.

At the end of the eighteenth century there were accusations that the florists' feasts were drinking parties not serious gardening occasions. But by the nineteenth century John Loudon noted that florists' societies were widespread. As more professional gardeners were employed, the societies became general horticultural societies instead of focusing on one particular flower, for instance, the Royal South London Floricultural Society, and the Ipswich and East England Horticultural Society.

Women did not figure very much in the records of the florists' societies. Only in 1872 did the Paisley Florists decide women could be admitted to the annual general meeting so that 'the members and their wives and sweethearts may enjoy a dance'. Presumably the wives and sweethearts were there in the background, watering plants, helping to wire them for shows, making tea and helpful suggestions, and sometimes, as a privilege, admitted to the feasts.

Since the florists' societies began, there has been a plethora of gardening clubs. The most well known, the arbiter of gardening tastes and interests in Britain, is the Royal Horticultural Society. At various times in its history it has been accused of being an exclusive club for gentlemen with wooded estates; stuffy, conservative, and so on. Now in its heyday, with an expanding membership and secure budget, it can risk a little more self-examination, and there is sometimes a hint of controversy at the A.G.M. – on the format of its monthly magazine the *Garden*, for instance. Its council, its executive and its medallists are predominantly male, although its membership is predominantly female, but this is typical of many large organizations.

Occasionally, gardening clubs were all-women clubs, for instance, the Women's Farm and Garden Association, founded nearly 100 years ago, is still in existence. Some of the clubs had a radical campaigning focus, such as Lady Eve Balfour's 'Soil Association', which was the forerunner of the organic gardening movement. Many of the societies are direct inheritors of the florists' societies' traditions; the delphinium society, the iris society and so on, each with their systems of showing and judging. From giant leeks to multi-coloured carnations, there are rules and regulations as to what constitutes a prize specimen; becoming a judge is a minor accolade. Many of these clubs or societies are affiliated to the R.H.S. which in turn is their collective voice.

Other clubs are local gardening clubs, of which one example is the garden at Harlow Carr in Harrogate, North Yorkshire. Harlow Carr Gardens was originally a 30-acre site leased from Harrogate Council. The prime mover behind its establishment was Colonel Hoare Grey (one-time gardening mentor of Vita Sackville-West), who had retired to the north and wanted a display garden for the Northern Horticultural Society, in which to grow plants that thrived in northern climates. Colonel Grey was a member of Harrogate Council, and had a brisk military approach to problem solving. Friends of his were commandeered to donate plants, and lend their gardeners to dig the site; he published a bi-monthly newsletter, most of which he wrote himself. In 1950 Mr Hare, the first head gardener, was appointed; after him Geoffrey Smith took up the post. Gradually the garden expanded to 68 acres. In 1983 a grant from the Countryside Commission enabled the garden society to convert a bath house into a study centre and library, and to fund 50 per cent of the cost of employing an education officer. In 1986 a plant centre and tearoom were added, then an administration block.

Philippa Rakusen was one of the people persuaded by Colonel Grey to volunteer her services to the garden, and she has been with Harlow Carr in various guises ever since. She recollects 'being absolutely mad about flowers' as a small child but followed a traditional pattern of marriage and family life. In her thirties, with her children beginning to grow up, she joined one of the specialist groups at Harlow Carr and was asked to list all the rhododendrons which had been donated. She worked with Barbara Clough, a slightly older woman, who was looking after elderly parents. Barbara was keen to have work outside the home but work and a career were unacceptable in her milieu, and marriage had not been an option; unless you were very beautiful or very determined your chances of marriage were very slight after the casualties of the First World War. Gardening was her outlet. Together, the two women took on more voluntary jobs, checking the woody plants, labelling, collecting and distributing seeds. They were invited to join various gardening committees, and then on to the council of Harlow Carr. When Barbara died in the 1970s Philippa Rakusen was devastated. Gradually, she collected another group of women around her who took on all the jobs she and Barbara had once done. It was a social occupation as well as a horticultural one:

> We were all in our forties, our children were going away . . . horticulture was the only profession where amateurs like us were accepted.

Finally, Philippa Rakusen became Director of Harlow Carr, a voluntary post, and has argued, reluctantly, for more professionalization. Many of the changes at Harlow Carr – the education centre, a playground, a museum and demonstration beds, including one of vegetables from the Asian subcontinent – are examples of changes she has pushed through. She is proud of her record but does not see herself as a pioneer: 'Middle-aged, middle-class women like me are a dying race . . . women now have to earn a living.'

Philippa Rakusen's own garden is a woodland garden. It is romantic; plants grow in rich and heady profusion, within the sheltering circle of the trees. Yet it is also a working garden, with three compost heaps and assorted sheds behind the house. Philippa Rakusen is pleasant, relaxed, easy-going and unassertive, a domesticated woman who has found pleasure, friendship and fulfilment in her gardening activities.

As well as local clubs, there are thriving national clubs, each with a particular mission; the Alpine Garden Society, whose leading spirit for some time was the cyclamen grower Doris Saunders; the Hardy Plant Society; the National Council for the Conservation of Plants and Gardens; and the Cottage Garden Society are the most well known. Their plant stalls and newsletters crop up not only at R.H.S. shows but in all sorts of unlikely venues. The Garden History Society, vigorously run by Mavis Batey, and the Tradescant Trust unearth fragments of history, piecing together plans, plantlists, letters,

Philippa Rakusen at home in her Yorkshire garden.

Harlow Carr garden, founded by Colonel Hoare Grey for the Northern Horticultural Society as a showpiece for plants which prefer colder climates.

diaries, and even researching old gardening tools, to recreate a picture of gardens which have long since disappeared.

The Hardy Plant Society was first formed in 1910 but it did not survive. It was then reincarnated in 1956, when it was launched by Alan Bloom. It led a rickety existence until 1961; it had 220 members but running it on a voluntary basis was an onerous task. The situation was saved by Miss Pole and Barbara White, the Chairman and Secretary respectively, who built up the organization. Its aims are:

> . . . to advance the culture, study, and improvement of herbaceous plants other than rock-plants . . . and to preserve older, rarer and lesser known hardy plants and varieties from being forgotten and lost to cultivation.

The society received its biggest boost from the publication of the *Plant Finder*, an alphabetical guide to locating more than 40,000 plants which are for sale in Britain. The list is a small triumph of marketing; with just a little cross-referencing, plant hunters can indulge in cross-country chases for plants, as only obsessionals know how. Every small nursery that makes an original discovery gets an advertising boost. The *Plant Finder* was originally compiled by Nottingham members of the society but has now become a publication in its own right.

In 1987, Jean Sambrook became General Secretary, continuing until the first paid administrator took over in 1992. She has steered the organization through a membership rise of 2000 to 8000. She works full-time as a middle-school technician but describes herself as a frustrated gardener. She remembers having an interest in gardening from the earliest age, spending sixpence a week on antirrhinums and pansies from Woolworth. She now runs a gardening club at her school, which also houses one of the national collections. Like many of the other women in this book, she began as a flower arranger, but found flower arranging too competitive, 'a world of ladies with time on their hands, some of whom were a bit ungracious when they lost'. Instead, she worked with the school children to build up a collection of lychnis. The children entered a conservation competition and won £2000, which was used to build the school greenhouse. This work has all been a labour of love, at school and at home. 'When I went on holiday I had to take a typewriter with me.' She is praised by other members of the society for her dedication, 'the most efficient woman I know'.

Efficiency is also the hallmark of Jane Taylor, who started the system of national collections of plants. She was a businesswoman, and had gardened as a child but had done very little gardening since. When she married, she moved with her husband in 1974 to a 'bleak and unappealing landscape', two acres of land, mainly slag from an almost defunct coal-mining industry. She decided to turn it into a garden, despite the advice of local people who said it was unworkable. She thought, 'I can't look at ghastly nothingness for the rest of my days', and with her husband cleared the site, fenced the land, added humus to the soil, and planted grass and daffodils. From this beginning with a pick and a mattock, the garden became a small paradise, full of unusual plants, cleverly arranged. Jane Taylor wrote:

> After years spent in the back-biting world of business it has been a refreshment to the soul to find ourselves, albeit on the fringes only, part of the warm and friendly gardening world.

On the strength of this gardening début, Jane and her husband were offered Coleton Fishacre Garden in Devon, by the National Trust in 1982. This had belonged to Rupert D'Oyly Carte, once filled with tender shrubs, but badly neglected and run down. They undertook the garden restoration and replanting. At the same time Jane Taylor, who was a member of the National Council for the Conservation of Plants and Gardens, became involved in the movement to start up collections of a particular genus or group of plants on one site, rather like a living museum. The national collections of kniphofias and watsonias were housed at Coleton Fishacre, and Jane Taylor wrote about some of the other national collections in *Collecting Garden Plants*.

The national collections are now organized from the R.H.S. gardens at Wisley in Surrey but in the beginning the system was run on a voluntary basis. 'At first almost anyone was welcomed with open arms . . . now we are more critical, we want the collections up to scratch.' The scheme provides guidance on record keeping, labelling, preparation of herbarium material, research and identification. Collection holders are expected to undertake some basic research about the plants, to find out about their historical origins, and to be aware of the constant problems about nomenclature and new varieties. The national collections are held by individuals, by gardening and other organizations – heathers at Harlow Carr, lychnis at Jean Sambrook's school – by nurseries, and by local authorities. There are several hundred collections, and Wisley publishes a guide to them.

RIGHT
Sophie Hughes holds one of the national collection of pinks. Her garden was 'a large bramble patch' when she and her husband first took it over.

FAR RIGHT
Coldham in Kent, with its unusual alpines, was another garden brought in to the National Garden Scheme. Its plant-sale – also part of the Scheme – is a magnet for visitors.

When Jane Taylor's husband died, she did not want to continue at Coleton Fishacre on her own. She decided she was 'essentially an urban animal' and moved back to London. In her late forties, she has remarried, and converted to the Muslim faith, and is known also as Saba Risaluddin. She has an unusual dual career: still producing her exceptionally well-researched and superbly written gardening books (even though her garden is now a window box filled with plants from the local garden centre); and also promoting inter-faith and equal opportunities issues. With her present husband she is a co-founder of the Calamus Foundation, a registered charity to promote understanding between Jews, Muslims and Christians, and is a Vice-chair of the Islamic Human Rights Group.

The national collection of pinks is held by Sophie Hughes. Like Jane Taylor, she is also a dual-career woman; a gardener and writer in her own time; and in the daytime, a social work manager. Fifteen years ago she and her husband moved from London to a 'large bramble patch' in Herefordshire. She knew very little about gardening, 'no visual imagination at all', but wanted to live in the country in order to raise a family. Her husband shaped the layout of the garden; she planted it and became interested in pinks, partly as an intellectual exercise, since their genealogy and history is so complicated and can be traced right back to the florists' feasts, partly because she thought they were so beautiful. She was inspired by Jane Taylor to take on the national collection.

Sophie Hughes had two children, and the pinks became an absorbing hobby; 'the world of lunatic gardeners' an antidote to the constraints of motherhood and domesticity. She exchanged plants, sought out old varieties, receiving 'shaky letters from elderly people' about long-lost treasures. She was given cuttings, wrote a book about pinks and carnations, and started up a small nursery. Publicity too early on in a colour supplement led to a flood of orders – 6000 letters, all of which she eventually managed to answer. Friends and other young mothers came to help, and the opportunity to sit and talk while propagating and dispatching the plants was therapeutic for the women involved.

The garden became well known, and was opened to the public. It was cleverly laid out and planted, and had a sunken garden, and a large pond with

a grotto underneath it. Unlike many gardens, it has also remained a children's playspace. A small mound with an arch at the end of the garden became a bike track for her son and his friends, who would cycle furiously over the top of it, and bounce down across the grass. Many visitors came; Sir Roy Strong, another gardening fanatic who lives locally, visited and was entranced by some skittles left on a step after the children were playing, mistaking them for a modernist sculpture.

Eventually, Sophie Hughes decided to return to her professional career; she and her husband reversed roles, and he now stays at home and manages the nursery. While at work she is discreet about her gardening activities but feels that the two sides of her life are complementary and that the stresses of work are dissipated in the pleasures and labour of the garden.

The most popular garden 'club' of all is the National Gardens Scheme. Under the Scheme private gardens are opened to the public, usually one or two days a year, sometimes more often, and the money raised goes to charity. Some gardens provide teas and plant sales; some of the small nurseries started off with open-day plant stalls. Visiting gardens provides an opportunity to see how other gardeners handle plants, to be inspired by new practical ideas about garden design, and simply to have an afternoon out with tea. From small beginnings in 1927, there are now over 3000 gardens in the scheme, which is organized on a countywide basis. *Gardens of England and Wales*, the 'Yellow Book' as it is known to acolytes, offers a short description of each of them. Each county has a county organizer, who visits gardens and encourages gardeners to take part, and administers the Scheme locally. The Scheme provides an opportunity to compare domestic gardens and offers a different category of visits from those to stately homes or the National Trust gardens, where the scale of the enterprise is beyond most people's means. It is overwhelmingly a women's organization although not deliberately or exclusively, and has some notable exceptions; but in practice it is mainly run by women, for women visiting other women's gardens. Vita Sackville-West, who first opened Sissinghurst to the public under the Scheme, wrote of her women visitors, '. . . homely souls . . . who will pore over a label, taking notes in a penny notebook'. Men, when they come, often appear to be 'in tow', as passive and sometimes unwilling chauffeurs or escorts!

Kent is one of the counties where the Scheme has grown and developed. The previous county organizer, Carolyn Hardy, scouted enthusiastically for every kind of interesting garden, whatever its size or scope, whether it specialized in begonias, alpines, rhododendrons or other plants. She persuaded many initially reluctant gardeners to take part in the Scheme and argued that small gardens as well as large ones had much to offer visitors, and that plantsmanship could be discovered in all sorts of odd corners. The present Kent organizer, Elizabeth Fleming, has carried on with the tradition, adding more gardens each year. It is this kind of involvement and energy which has helped the Scheme expand, lose its vicar's tea-party image, and achieve its present status as a national hobby.

Jeane Rankin is a London gardener who has just joined the scheme and opened her garden for the first time. She is a partially disabled gardener, keen to share her knowledge.

> I want to open my garden to share with people . . . it seems silly for just me to enjoy it . . . I want others to look . . . it will bring some people who are dead keen on plants and can talk plants to me, which I don't have otherwise. There's nobody around as keen as I am.

She created the garden herself, despite increasingly crippling arthritis. She had some help with the building and construction. She did not want fully raised beds, which she thought would highlight her disability, but compromised with slightly raised sections. She likes foliage plants, and is careful about colours.

> You need a garden to please your eye . . . there's also a very nice solitude that comes with gardening, quite different from other kinds of solitude . . . it's beautiful and I can never get over what plants do . . . you forget any pains you've got.

Jeane Rankin likes raising money too, the charitable side of the operation. As in so many of the gardens which are open, family and friends rally round to prepare and help serve the teas, which double the takings, and give a party atmosphere to the event.

Discussion, research, conservation, lobbying, solidarity and sheer pleasure; the society of gardeners today is not so far removed from the days of florists' feasts. Gardening is still a celebratory event.

CHAPTER TEN

LIFE AND CREATIVITY

Aquotation from a homely early American writer on gardening, Minnie Aumonier, 'When the world wearies, and society ceases to satisfy, there is always the garden,' highlights one of the themes of gardening, that the garden is a refuge and a sanctuary from the bruisings of life. The garden is not only a place of retreat; it is a positive arena, a place to recreate a vision of nature, to experiment, to control, to collect, a space to decorate. There is, of course, no generalization which holds good for all women, or which predicts and distinguishes the way men and women garden. Women are often more housebound than men, and the garden is an opportunity to indulge their genius on their doorstep without being thought unwomanly or overtly challenging conventions about the role and place of women. Even this situation is changing, as increasing numbers of women work to earn their own living.

This was never intended as a feminist book, and many of the women described in it would deny any interest or connection with feminist concerns, but researching stories about women gardeners inevitably becomes a social quest. Why were women invisible? Why are they so visible now? Are they gaining the recognition they deserve? The case for gardening to be regarded

A view of York Gate,
the Yorkshire garden which combines a clever use
of objects with skilled planting.

as an art appears in all kinds of garden writing. The claim that it is a woman's art, a domain where women both predominate and excel, is more complex. All the women who appear in this book, and the hundreds more who deserve to, are confirmation that a small revolution has occurred, and that the recognition of individual achievements is also a reflection of wider social change.

This last chapter looks at some contemporary gardens, a mixture of great and small. They are arbitrarily selected – for how else can it be done – and they represent a fraction of what exists. They owe no obvious allegiance to any style, they are not dependent on lavish incomes or connections, but they reflect the exuberance, the refinement, the commitment and the imagination of their women owners.

Lucy Gent is a London gardener, whose long narrow garden behind a Georgian terrace has attracted much admiration. She was an academic, a lecturer in English who became increasingly obsessed with plants and garden design. Like so many others, she was inspired by Sissinghurst, 'a real eye-

Lucy Gent in her long narrow London garden. She has a landscape artist's concern with space and proportion, as well as being an obsessive plantswoman.

opener', but also acknowledges more immediate influences. Her next-door neighbour, a Latvian translator, had tried in her own garden to recreate some of her childhood memories of Latvian meadows, and this style of gardening, and reliance on herbaceous materials, had made Lucy reconsider her own preferences. 'I was brought up on shrubs, but through Ruth I began to exploit the herbaceous side.' Another influence, her gardening mentor, was Valerie Finnis, whose superb handling of plants is still a source of admiration.

Lucy Gent became interested in garden design, in the overall balance of plants and materials, and in the architectural challenge of her long oblong of a garden. Landscape architecture and horticulture have an uneasy relationship in Britain, the architects being seen as cavalier about plants, and the plantsmen dismissive of design. Lucy Gent tries to straddle both approaches. She is concerned with vertical and horizontal tensions, with volume, with the appearance of the garden from different angles, from different heights. Looking down from a window she notices the foliage canopies, 'I like the way shapes flow along . . . increasingly I think large leaves look wonderful.' She has some very special and treasured plants, and a few very brightly coloured ones but increasingly she is concerned with leaf shape and colour. 'I dislike the green of gardens, there is too much mid-green.'

One of her gardening friends is Thelma Kay, who has a small L-shaped garden around her bungalow in a suburb of Manchester. The garden is a treasure-trove of rare plants, many collected by Thelma Kay herself on trips abroad, and few of which normally survive outdoors, even in the south of England. Thelma Kay was a nurse and, by her own admission, 'didn't know a thing about gardening'. She grew her own vegetables on an allotment, and gradually became interested in plants. She, too, was inspired by Sissinghurst, and recollects her first visit there. She met Vita Sackville-West, who said to her, 'You're a bit young for gardening, it comes with age you see', and then asked where Thelma was from. When she heard that it was Manchester, she threw up her hands in horror, 'just like that with her hands, as if to say nobody can garden in Manchester'.

Thelma Kay became a Manchester councillor, a J.P., and as a part-time hobby took a City and Guild's course on hatmaking. She started making extravagant hats, which sold well and financed her gardening trips abroad.

'I save up the money and I just go – Kashmir, the Galapagos, Ecuador, Japan, Australia and Brazil.' She is now 70 but still makes hats, and has one to match every outfit she owns. As well as travelling she reads voraciously. Her own garden is thoroughly dug and manured (with elephant dung from Bellevue zoo on one occasion), and she has created numerous small micro-climates, with different aspects or different soils which enable her plants to survive. The fencing is concrete, which holds in the warmth of the sun, and an extension to the bungalow provides more south-facing niches. In winter, the plants are covered with old clothes for protection.

All her plants are carefully grown and staked and pruned; it is an exceptionally well-ordered garden as well as one which overflows with plants. One section leads neatly into another; the small lawn is perfect. Even now, Thelma Kay does all the gardening herself; the only help she has ever had was with erecting the fence and making a stone path. She gardens to please herself, continually adding and changing: 'I have a constant vision of what things might be like.' She propagated many of her own plants and for a while ran a small nursery, but the flow of visitors was too much and so after four years she gave it up. She still has many visitors from garden clubs and societies, who come to see the unbelievable sight of tropical plants flourishing in a damp northern climate.

Across the Pennines in Leeds, there are another two well-known and much visited gardens. Sybil Spencer describes her one-acre garden as 'an orchard with pool, an arbour, miniature pinetum, dell with stream, folly, nutwalk, peony bed, iris borders, fern border, herb garden, summerhouse, alley, white and silver garden, pavement maze and vegetable garden'. This may sound impossibly crammed, as only the English know how, but it is not. It is a magical garden, with one theme dissolving into the next; strange antiques outlined or softened by plants; a garden which even on a misty wet autumn day is full of shapes and surprises, of eye-catching vignettes.

The garden was created with her husband and son. Sadly, they have both died but Sybil Spencer maintains the feel and appearance of the garden as they knew it. Her husband 'laid out the bare bones of the garden', and her son Robin filled it with objects.

> I would say what I would like. A herb garden, a white and silver garden, a pool, and one or other of my menfolk would decide where it had to go and how it should be designed . . . I was the plantswoman, shrubs, trees, perennials.

Her son taught her about placing objects in the garden.

> Robin had a wonderful faculty for finding things, antiques that he thought could have a place in the garden, and he was a very slow thinker, nothing was put on squared paper, but he had a faculty for doing free drawing and he'd submit it to me and he'd say, 'What do you think of this, Mum?' . . . It was always right so I usually said go ahead . . . but he was in danger of overdecorating the garden. He couldn't stop designing, creating . . . I put him a bit right there.

Like so many others, Sybil Spencer is self-taught, reading, experimenting, visiting other gardens. Although she had always had a garden, it was only at York Gate that she became obsessed. Weeding became her favourite hobby, and gardening a daily activity. 'It's a poor sort of day when I don't do some sort of gardening.' And like other women, she relishes the contacts and social life that gardening brings.

> I've made so many gardening friends! It's marvellous and nearly everyone brings one a plant or something they know I'm fond of, or chocolates or biscuits. They're most generous. They're thrilled to bits if they can bring me a plant that they think I haven't got.

Frieda Brown is another Yorkshire gardener, with a tiny, irregularly shaped garden behind her council house on an estate on the outskirts of Leeds. At the age of 50, when she first moved to the house, she had never handled a spade. Her childhood had been spent in the East End of London, and her earliest consciousness of flowers was of convolvulus growing through the concrete and twining around the fences. She had trained at art college, her husband Joe was an engineer, and when they came to their new house in 1963 both were in full-time work.

It was a local competition, organized by Leeds Housing Department and the *Yorkshire Evening Post*, 'Flowers for Leeds', which was their first milestone. They designed the garden around the idea of 'flowing lines, water and stone'. In 1972 they won a silver cup, which spurred them to greater effort. They acquired an extra piece of land at the bottom of the garden, and they joined the Northern Horticultural Society, and visited Harlow Carr Gardens, which was their second milestone. They began to read gardening books, and installed an 8 foot by 6 foot greenhouse for propagation and overwintering. The third milestone was joining the Hardy Plant Society.

> The secretary came and gave an illustrated talk. It left me reeling and staggering . . . there have been wonderful meetings and discussions.

As their gardening horizons grew, so did the garden. Joe was the labourer and supplier, scavenging all sorts of unusual materials for the garden – stone, wrought iron and marble. Frieda was the plantswoman and designer. She looks smart for work or for visitors but, in the garden, 'I look like Woodbine Lizzie, I wear cut-down trousers and I never wear gloves.' She specializes in clematis, and grows more than 60 different kinds, as well as other climbers such as *Passiflora caerulea* and the notoriously difficult *Rhodochiton atrosanguineum*. There are two pools, and alpine troughs and a rockery. There is a good collection of ferns including the native tatting fern. Part of a neighbour's garden is used as plant hospital and nursery bed, in exchange for maintenance of the rest. It is a very cleverly designed garden and by using different levels, and linking materials, stone walls and paths, ornamentation, statues and seating, all accentuated by the planting, it gives the illusion of being a much greater space than it is.

The garden is stunning but, even if it were not, the pleasures that have come from gardening surpass all else.

> It's a wonderful, exciting sort of occupation – I can't imagine how I ever lived before I took up gardening . . . women tend to have delicacy and

imagination . . . planting seeds is like giving birth, it's almost erotic sometimes . . . when I retired I missed the communication with people but through the garden I've made the most marvellous friends.

In Somerset, Sandra and Nori Pope have created a very different garden, a herbaceous border on a grand scale, following to the letter the precepts of Gertrude Jekyll. They are both Canadians, who have come to Britain because, 'We wanted to come to a country where people garden seriously.' Nori, a

BELOW
Sandra Pope
weeding the red
and purple section
of the long curved
herbaceous border
at Hadspen.

LEFT
Frieda and Joe
Brown in their tiny
Leeds garden. They
entered the Leeds
Housing
Department/
Yorkshire Post
'Flowers for Leeds'
competition, won a
silver cup and never
looked back.

LEFT
Papaver orientale 'Mrs
Merrow's Plum',
one of the most
beautiful of all
poppies, discovered
by Sandra and Nori
Pope, and grown in
the purple spectrum
of the border.

botanist, had a nursery in Vancouver which specialized in old shrub roses and Sandra, who had no gardening qualifications, was a student at his evening class on gardening. After they married they visited England, hoping to spend some time looking at gardens, and possibly to find somewhere to rent. Jane Taylor introduced them to Hadspen, once the garden of Penelope Hobhouse, but by then a little run-down and neglected. They decided to rent the walled garden, which up until then had not been used to grow flowers, and to restore part of the original garden, including the water-tank pool. 'It was a great romantic tangle . . . we had to do a lot of radical pruning and chainsaw work.'

Sandra Pope concentrated on the walled area, a 765-yards long curved wall with a wide bed in front of it. She followed through the colours of the spectrum, starting with yellows and greens (which carried on from her husband's borders in another part of the garden), through blues and violets to the hot scarlets and reds.

> Even this space isn't enough. To go through the colour transitions without being blocky and chunky, but to flow through the colours, meant that we had to make compromises.

Every single plant in the border has been carefully placed, to complement and enhance the colour tones of its neighbours. The subtlety of the combinations is exquisite, from the pure ice-blue tones of irises through to a rich plum-coloured oriental poppy juxtaposed with apricot lupins.

The garden is open to visitors for part of the week, and there is a small nursery attached. They attract garden tours.

> We take it in turns to be head gardener. Nori knows distances, sizes and shapes and shadows. I don't think in those terms. I'm terrible at straight lines and distant things. But I think women have a better sense of colour than men do . . . We discuss it endlessly.

On a still grander scale is Nancy Lancaster. Now in her nineties, she is one of the grand dames of gardening this century. Although born and brought up in the United States, Nancy Lancaster was partly educated in Europe. As a young woman she used to make regular visits to Cliveden to stay with her aunt,

Nancy Astor, the first woman M.P. to take her seat in Parliament. She settled in England in 1926 as the wife of Ronald Tree, who was soon to become a Conservative M.P. They rented Kelmarsh, a large Georgian house in Northamptonshire. Their first real home in England was at Ditchley Park in Oxfordshire, where they regularly entertained Winston Churchill and his political retinue during the Second World War, when Chequers was considered too conspicuous to German night-bombers. Sir Geoffrey Jellicoe, the landscape architect, was employed to recreate the formal garden, and he designed a terrace closed by a curving wall of water in the style of a Tuscan villa. He remembers the grandeur of one particular party that was held there when Ronald Tree's half-brother, Peter Beatty, won the Derby in 1938.

> They invited 2000 guests . . . and Nancy insisted that all the women should be dressed either in red or white . . . and the gentlemen in black, and the spectacle of this moving in the garden was really lovely . . . there was a temporary pavilion on the terrace designed by Oliver Messel, and there was music everywhere . . . I defy anybody to do it better . . . they made money at the races and [blew] it at this party . . . in grand style.

Interior decorating was an acceptable outlet for a woman of Nancy Lancaster's background and she always had a feel for houses and how they should look. She managed to combine the formality of the English country house with a certain informality and flair inside, and introduced the American notion of comfort for the first time in bedrooms and bathrooms. At the end of the war she became a partner in the firm, of Colefax and Fowler. Stanley Falconer, the present director of the firm, describes the discreet nature of her contribution:

> She did not deal with clients, as such, at all, but she brought in through her friends influential clients to this business. Her input on taste was immeasurable.

She designed part of the premises of the firm, in a style which Stanley Falconer describes as trail-blazing, and 'copied everywhere', with yellow gloss walls, two layers of looped silk shantung curtains, each a slightly different shade of yellow, hung from gilded curtain poles. In her home at Haseley Court, she used hand-painted copies of eighteenth-century wallpaper (and in one room, the original) and favoured gilded and painted furniture, and needlepoint furnishings. In a *Vogue* article she is described as having,

> a talent for placing possessions and an instinctive feeling for furniture, almost a private understanding with beautiful things as though she could call to them and they would come to her.

At the age of 96, with many Cecil Beaton photographs behind her, she is still stylishly dressed and colour co-ordinated, in yellows, or blue, or black and

Nancy Lancaster watering her red and yellow border
in earlier days at Haseley Court.

RIGHT
The eight-spoked box wheel,
with Kent cobblestone paths, at Haseley Court.

white, each outfit matched with a hat worn at a rakish angle. Two large elegant dogs keep her company and add to the image. Her voice is deep and gravelly, and she laughs a great deal – sometimes at herself. She has abundant charm and is remembered with affection by almost everyone who knows her.

Born in Virginia, her first garden was at Mirador, her grandfather's house nestling under the Blue Ridge Mountains. 'The mountains seemed to come down to the garden like blue soot . . . and the earth was a sort of red clay.' In summer, the garden was hot and dry and arid, but the long spring and

autumn seasons were enchanting. She remembers 'the tumbles of honeysuckles that you walked through and you saw the mountains at the end of it'.

She had always been conscious of the continuity of house and garden, but Ditchley made her particularly aware of the architecture of the house, and the need to complement it by the landscaping of the garden. 'I can feel the atmosphere of a house and what type of garden it was . . . I have more of a feeling for a house than for people . . .'

In 1955 Nancy Lancaster, as she had become, discovered Haseley Court in Oxfordshire. It dated back to 1703, with many subsequent additions, but the garden was first described in 1540 by John Leyland.

> Little Haseley . . . hath a right fair mansion place and marvellous fair walks topiarii operis and orchards and pools.

The house had been untouched for many years, but the sixteenth-century topiary garden, in the shape of a chessboard, had been replanted in 1850, and was still being clipped by a local gardener, even though the rest of the ground was full of nettles and generally neglected. She was impressed by the amount of land.

> I'm an awful land snob. I love land! And I'm terribly impressed, you can show me an old drunk, if he owns land I can't help making up to him. Isn't that extraordinary? I mean it isn't money or titles at all . . . but land, I've got a real lust for land! I can never have enough land.

Eventually Nancy Lancaster bought Haseley Court, had it renovated inside, and with her first romantic garden at Virginia in mind, began to design the garden. The topiary chesspieces, of box and yew, were underplanted with santolina and lavender, and the chessboard hemmed with alternate yew and portuguese laurel. Beyond it, across to the Chiltern hills, stretches the beautiful empty Oxfordshire countryside.

Geoffrey Jellicoe helped again by designing a raised terrace for the Queen Anne frontage of the house. Soft grey aromatic shrubs are planted up against the sheltering walls of the house. A double avenue of limes has recently been planted to replace the avenue of chestnuts, which now stretches from the front of the house across a ha-ha to the horizon.

The remains of a fifteenth-century moat were turned into a canal, ending in a fountain pool with a small cascade, the home to ducks and golden orfe. The canal sits at the end of a woodland garden with trees underplanted with hellebores and lilies and spring bulbs.

From a hayfield Nancy Lancaster made an enclosed garden, divided into four with a New England-style summerhouse where the paths intersected. One quarter-garden is a parterre, an eight-spoked box wheel with curlicues, with walks of flint cobble winding between the low box hedges; another is a croquet lawn with old and climbing roses on grey-blue painted wooden lattice pyramids; the third is a circular pottager with sea kale, irises, fruit and other vegetables; and the fourth a lawn bounded by borders of shrubs and flowers – lavender, fuchsia and aquilegia. This garden is walled on two sides; on the remaining two sides there are long tunnels of pleached lime, again underplanted with bulbs, with the end of each tunnel marked with a striking statue or large pot.

Nancy Lancaster does not consider herself as a plantswoman. She admires old-fashioned flowers, honeysuckle, old roses, hollyhocks, poppies and foxgloves, and she likes the annuals and biennials to seed themselves – a style of gardening which requires some forbearance from the garden staff. The effect she aims at is a slight nostalgia: 'I like things to be a little sad, a little run-down.' The edge of a border should be 'like an old lady's petticoat'. This is a style which her friend Imogen Taylor describes as 'shabby chic'. Many of her plants were originally bought from nearby Waterperry, where she used to visit Miss Havergal and encourage the eager young Valerie Finnis. Despite her staff of gardeners, she describes herself as a hands-on gardener.

> I remember getting up at five and six in the morning. I could hardly wait to get my hands in the dirt. I enjoyed it. This is the fun of a garden I think, doing it yourself.

Some years ago Nancy Lancaster sold the house and grounds. She now lives in the adjoining coach house but retains her walled garden. Nowadays, her mobility is limited; she uses an electric wheelchair, and she can no longer bend and weed and deadhead flowers, but she retains her zest and her memories.

I've enjoyed tremendously all the houses that I've lived in and I feel no regrets at all . . . I think I was frightfully lucky to be able to do what I wanted to do. So many people love lovely things and never get a chance to have them so I don't feel I can complain.

These women gardeners are a tiny selection of those that might have been included. Their backgrounds are dissimilar, and so are their gardens, but they share obsessions; plants, propagation, choosing, arranging, displaying, cultivating, creating a grand design. They belong to societies and gardening organizations; they lecture, judge, talk and write about their hobby; they are absorbed in it. For all of them, the garden has been a source of friendship as well as a source of creativity, a haven and an inspiration. Few activities are so spellbinding. Perhaps we should end as we began, with a quotation from the American writer and poet, Alice Walker:

> My mother adorned with flowers whatever shabby house we were forced to live in. Whatever she planted grew as if by magic, and because of her creativity with flowers, even my memories of poverty are seen through a screen of blooms – sunflowers, petunias, roses, delphiniums, verbena and so on . . . a garden so magnificent with life and creativity, that to this day perfect strangers ask to stand or walk amongst my mother's art.

Haseley: the view from the blue-painted summerhouse down the borders of what was once an old hayfield. All the garden furnishings are blue. Nancy Lancaster jokes that white furniture is 'aspirin coloured'.

BIBLIOGRAPHY

AMHERST Alicia *A History of Gardening in England* John Murray, 1910 edition.

ARCHITECTURAL ASSOCIATION *Miss Gertrude Jekyll 1843–1932 Gardener* Catalogue to A.A. exhibition, 1981.

BLACKWELL Elizabeth *A Curious Herbal*, 1737.

BLUNT Wilfrid *The Art of Botanical Illustration* Collins, 1950.

BRAY Lys de *Fantastic Garlands* Blandford Press, 1982.

BRAY Lys de *Cottage Garden Year* Grange Books, 1991.

BROWN Jane *Vita's Other World* Viking, 1985.

BROWN Jane *Eminent Gardeners: Some People of Influence and Their Gardens, 1880–1980* Viking, 1990.

CHATTO Beth *The Dry Garden* J. M. Dent, 1978.

CHATTO Beth *The Damp Garden* J. M. Dent, 1982.

CHATTO Beth *Plant Portraits* J. M. Dent, 1985.

CHATTO Beth *Garden Notebook* J. M. Dent, 1988.

CHIVERS Susan and WOLOSZYNSKA Suzanne *The Cottage Garden: Margery Fish at East Lambrook Manor* John Murray, 1990.

COLVIN Brenda *Land and Landscape* Murray, 1970.

DESMOND Ray *Loudon and Nineteenth Century Horticultural Journalism* in ed. Elisabeth B. MacDougall: *John Claudius Loudon and the Early Nineteenth Century in Britain.* Dumbarton Oaks Colloquium, 1980.

DUTHIE Ruth *Florist's Flowers and Societies* Shire Garden History, 1988.

EARLE Mrs C. M. *Pot-Pourri from a Surrey Garden*, 1897, re-issued Century, 1984.

ELLIOTT Brent *Victorian Gardens* Batsford, 1986.

EVELYN John *The Diary of John Evelyn* ed. E. S. Beer, Oxford University Press, 1959.

FESTING Sally *Gertrude Jekyll* Viking, 1991.

FISH Margery *We Made a Garden* Collingridge, 1956, re-issued Faber, 1983.

FLETCHER H. R. *The Story of the Royal Horticultural Society 1804–1968* Oxford University Press for R.H.S., 1969.

GERARD John *The Herball*, 1597.

GOULD Stephen Jay *The Flamingo's Smile* Penguin, 1985.

GREER Germaine *The Obstacle Race* Secker and Warburg, 1979.

HARVEY John *Early Nurserymen* Phillimore, 1974.

HARVEY Sheila, ed., *Reflections on Landscape: The Lives and Work of Six British Landscape Architects* (inc. Sylvia Crowe, Brenda Colvin) Gower, 1987.

HAYDEN Ruth *Mrs Delany, her Life and her Flowers* Colonnade Books in association with the British Museum, 1980.

HOBHOUSE Penelope *The Country Gardener* Phaidon, 1976.

HOBHOUSE Penelope *Colour in Your Garden* Collins, 1985.

HOBHOUSE Penelope *Garden Style* Frances Lincoln, 1988.

HOPE Frances *Notes and Thoughts on Gardens and Woodlands*, 1881.

HUGHES Sophie *Carnations and Pinks* Crowood Press, 1991.

HYLL Thomas (Dydymus Mountaine) *The Gardeners-Labyrinth*, 1577, re-issued, HILL Thomas *The Gardener's Labyrinth* ed. Richard Mabey, Oxford University Press, 1987.

JACKSON Maria E. *The Florist's Manual*, 1827.

JEKYLL Gertrude *A Gardener's Testament* ed. Francis Jekyll and G. C. Taylor, Country Life, 1937, re-issued Papermac, 1984.

JOHNSON Hugh, ed. *The Garden: A Celebration of One Thousand Years of British Gardening* Catalogue, Victoria & Albert Exhibition, 1979.

JOHNSON Louisa *Every Lady her own Flower Gardener*, 1837.

JOHNSON Louisa *Every Lady's Guide to her Own Greenhouse*, 1851.

LAWRENCE John *A New System of Agriculture, a Complete Body of Husbandry and Gardening*, 1726.

LAWRENCE Mary *A Collection of Roses from Nature*, 1799.

LAWSON William *Countrie Houswifes Garden*, 1617, re-issued *The Country House-wife's Garden* Breslich & Foss, 1983.

LIEVRE Audrey Le *Ellen Willmott of Warley Place* Faber and Faber, 1980.

LOUDON Jane *Instruction in Gardening for Ladies*, 1840.

LOUDON Jane *Ladies' Companion to the Flower-Garden* William Smith, 1841.

LOUDON Jane *The Ladies' Country Companion*, 1846.

LOUDON John Claudius *Encyclopedia of Gardening*, 1822.

MABEY Richard *The Flowering of Kew* Century, 1988.

MADDY Ursula *Waterperry: A Dream Fulfilled* Merlin Books, 1990.

MARSH Jan *Back to the Land: The Pastoral Impulse in England from 1880 to 1914* Quartet, 1982.

MASSINGHAM Betty *A Century of Gardeners* Faber and Faber, 1988.

MEE Margaret *In Search of Flowers of the Amazon Forest: Diaries of an English Artist*, ed. Tony Morrison, Nonesuch Expeditions, 1988.

MERIAN Maria Sybilla *The Wondrous Transformation of Caterpillars* Scholar Press, 1978.

MITFORD Mary Russell *Our Village*, 1832, re-issued Isis, 1991.

MITFORD Mary Russell *My Garden*, ed. Robyn Marsack, Sidgwick and Jackson, 1990.

MORIARTY Henrietta *Fifty Plates of Greenhouse Plants*, 1803.

MURRAY Charlotte *The British Garden*, 1799.

NORTH Marianne *A Vision of Eden: The Life and Work of Marianne North* Webb and Bower in association with the Royal Botanical Gardens, Kew, 1980.

PAGE Russell *The Education of a Gardener* Collins, 1962.

PARKINSON John *Paradisi in Sole Paradisus Terrestris* 1629, re-issued Dover, 1980.

PAVORD Anna *Garden Companion* Chatto and Windus, 1992.

PERENYI Eleanor *Green Thoughts: A Writer in the Garden* Allen Lane, 1981.

PERRY Frances *Water Gardening*, 1938, re-issued Avra Editions, 1985.

PRATT Anne *Flowers and Their Associations*, 1826.

PRATT Anne *Flowering Plants, Sedges and Ferns of Great Britain*, 1846.

RANSON Florence *British Herbs* Penguin, 1949.

READ Herbert *The Meaning of Art* Penguin, 1952.

ROBINSON William *The Wild Garden*, 1870, re-issued Century, 1983.

ROHDE Eleanor Sinclair *The Story of the Garden* The Medici Society, 1932, reprinted 1989.

ROSS-CRAIG Stella *Drawings of British Plants*, 31 vols., G Bell & Sons, 1962–3.

ROTHSCHILD Miriam and FARRELL C. *The Butterfly Gardener* Michael Joseph, 1968.

ROTHSCHILD Miriam *Dear Lord Rothschild* Hutchinson, 1983.

ROUSSEAU Jean-Jacques *Elementary Letters on Botany to a Lady*, 1785, re-issued as *Botany: A Study of Pure Curiosity* Michael Joseph, 1979.

SACKVILLE-WEST Vita *Garden Book* Michael Joseph, 1968.

SOCIETY OF GARDENERS *Catalogus Plantarum*, 1730.

STEARN William *Flower Artists of Kew* Herbert Press, 1990.

STEP Edward *Wayside and Woodland Blossoms*, 1895.

STRONG Roy *The Renaissance Garden in England* Thames and Hudson, 1979.

TAYLOR Jane *Collecting Garden Plants* J. M. Dent, 1988.

TEMPLE Sir William *Upon the Garden of Epicurus*, 1685.

TUSSER Thomas *A hundreth good pointes of husbandrie united to as many of good huswiferie*, 1573 edition, re-issued ed. Hartley, Country Life, 1931.

VEREY Rosemary *The Scented Garden* Michael Joseph/Marshall edition, 1981.

VEREY Rosemary and LEES-MILNE Alvida *The New Englishwoman's Garden* Chatto & Windus, 1987.

WAKEFIELD Priscilla *An Introduction to Botany*, 1796.

WALKER Alice *In Search of Our Mothers' Gardens* The Women's Press, 1984.

WILLMOTT Ellen *Warley Garden in Spring and Summer*, 1909.

PICTURE CREDITS

BBC Books would like to thank the following for providing photographs and for permission to reproduce copyright material. While every effort has been made to trace and acknowledge all copyright holders, we would like to apologise should there have been any errors or omissions.

Page 2 Royal Horticultural Society; **12** Mary Evans Picture Library; **14** Lord Rockley; **16** Giraudon/Bridgeman Art Library/Musée des Beaux-Arts, Lille; **18** Royal Horticultural Society; **20** Yale Centre for British Art Paul Mellon Collection; **24, 25 & 28** Royal Horticultural Society; **29** Royal Botanic Gardens, Kew; **33** Royal Horticultural Society; **38** Anne Jones; **42** (all) Royal Horticultural Society; **45** National Portrait Gallery; **48/49** Grosvenor Museum, Chester; **49 & 50** Royal Horticultural Society; **52t** Country Life; **52b** Mr. R. J. Berkeley; **54** Country Life; **56** National Trust Photo Library/Nick Meers; **58** Country Life; **60** Valerie Finnis; **61** National Trust Photo Library/Eric Crichton; **62** Country Life; **68** Penelope Hobhouse/BBC Photographic Unit/John Jefford; **70** National Portrait Gallery; **72** British Architectural Library/RIBA; **75** (both pictures) East Sussex County Libraries (Wolseley Collection); **77** University of Reading Library (Studley Collection Archive); **78** Royal Botanic Gardens, Kew; **81** Practical Gardening Magazine/Malcolm Birkitt; **82** Valerie Finnis; **83** Ursula Maddy; **88** Valerie Finnis; **89** Jan Baldwin; **98** Diany Binny; **108** Hugh Palmer; **109** BBC Photographic Unit/Robert Hill; **115** Royal Horticultural Society; **116/117** Bridgeman Art Library/Christopher Wood Gallery, London; **117** Royal Horticultural Society; **146** The Independent/George Wright; **150** Bridgeman Art Library/RHS; **151** National Portrait Gallery; **153** ET Archive/RHS; **154–161** (all) Royal Botanic Gardens, Kew; **164** (both) Valerie Finnis; **165** Richard Pink, Royal Studios, Wimborne; **167** (both) Marion & Tony Morrison; **172** Valerie Finnis; **176** Garden Picture Library/Steven Wooster; **180 & 185** BBC Photographic Unit/Robert Hill; **188** John Glover; **193t** George Wright; **193b** Photos Horticultural/Michael & Lois Warren; **196** Sunday Times/Alex Dufort; **197** John Glover; **212** Valerie Finnis.

All other photographs are by **Andrew Lawson**.

INDEX